A Scottish
NATURE
Diary

The Pass of Killiecrankie, in glowing autumn colours. *Scotland in Focus/ Roger Fox.*

A Scottish
NATURE
Diary

DOUGLAS WILLIS

JOHN DONALD PUBLISHERS Ltd
EDINBURGH

ISBN 0 85976 305 6

British Library Cataloguing in Publication Data

Willis, Douglas P.
A Scottish nature diary.
1. Scotland. Natural history
I. Title
508.411

Typeset by Pioneer Associates, Perthshire
Printed and Bound in Great Britain by
Cambus Litho, Nerston, East Kilbride

ACKNOWLEDGEMENTS

I should like to express my thanks to the following: Mrs M. Lingen-Hutton (quotations from the works of Violet Jacob); the Trustees of the Charles Murray Memorial Trust; Aberdeen University Press (Poems by J. C. Milne, 1963); A. Hunter (quotations from the works of Helen B. Cruickshank); and Flora Garry and Peter Buchan, in whose verses I have breathed the clear air of Buchan. Of the jacket illustrations, the one of the Blue Tit is by Roger Fox. The remainder, including the one on the back, are by Laurie Campbell.

Douglas Willis

CONTENTS

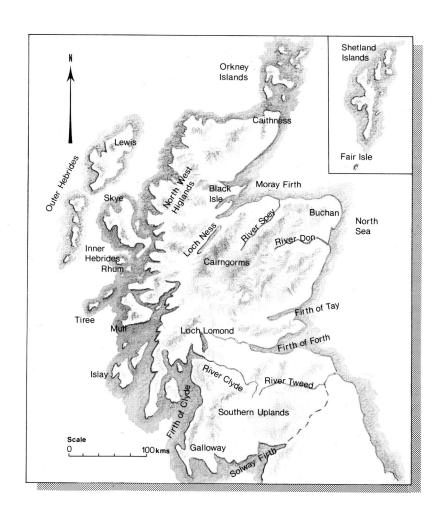

GEOGRAPHICAL FEATURES

Corrie on Beinn Dearg, Wester Ross, the grey face of winter outlined on its ice-ravaged face. *Douglas Willis.*

INTRODUCTION

*F*OR the past few years I have contributed a weekly nature diary to the *Ross-shire Journal.* My inspiration has been the area around my Black Isle home — the farmlands, forests and firths of this lovely northern setting, but I have tried also to capture the character of other parts of our Scottish country scene as I have travelled around.

For myself, it has been a discipline in noting the unfolding patterns of the living landscape, week by week, season by season. For my readers, it seems that it has been for some a weekly armchair experience of the countryside in familiar and sometimes less familiar settings; for others an encouragement to venture out and enjoy the country places for themselves. Nor have my countryside experiences been without their lighter moments, too, as will be evident, I hope, from some of the passages that follow.

As the years have passed and one season has merged into another, I have been able to share some classic countryside days. Equally, there have been many occasions when, through the kind of circumstances which rule most of our lives, it has not been possible to be out and about so much. At these times it has been necessary to focus on the ordinary, everyday ongoings of the natural world, frequently those which take place in the restricted setting of the garden. And yet, it is those ordinary observations on everyday wildlife happenings that have encouraged many of my readers to take another look at the apparently humdrum happenings round about them.

Published country diaries invariably consist of extract accounts from daily entries. As such they are a shared record of personal experiences, specific to particular moments in time. I have employed a certain licence in interpreting the term, attempting to broaden the interest and, hopefully, the practical value, for readers by allowing each month to reflect the kind of things that have occupied my countryside jottings over the years. It is offered, therefore, as a seasonal evocation of our country places; both a shared experience and a calendar of the kind of things that may be looked for and enjoyed month by month in our Scottish countryside.

Outlined in the frosty air of sunset, a lone tree provides its own striking contribution to the winter scene. *Douglas Willis.*

JANUARY

'Ilk happing bird, wee, helpless thing,
That in the merry months o' spring
Delighted me to hear thee sing,
What comes o' thee?
Whare wilt thou cower thy chittering wing,
An close thy ee?'

ROBERT BURNS

*J*ANUARY. A new year. Satisfying in the predictability of its seasonal rhythms, our Scottish countryside has an inbuilt thrawnness to its character as well. The month may open to a mildness that encourages an early budding, but it may just as likely usher in a spell of harsh weather cold enough to glaze even the seaside rock pools and crystallise the salt spray into baroque ice forms at the very edge of the tide.

Winter cave

Start of a new calendar year.

With the winter solstice past and the round of the year now turned, I find myself willing each early January day to seem just a little longer than the one that went before. I curse each afternoon of sullen cloud as an interruption in the progress towards the lengthening days. Whether I really perceive any difference at all at January's beginning is questionable, but the early birds can already sense the difference, and some are determined to say so.

Small wonder that the ancients went more than a little dotty over the solstice, for it was a pivotal point in the cycle of their year. As if to share in the ancients' sense of oneness with the progress of the countryside year, I find myself drawn each New Year's Day to a sea cave that lies a mile or two along the shore.

Behind a bracken-draped midden heap of shells once assiduously

3

gathered from the rock pools, the morning sun — when it deigns to penetrate the grey cloud veil — shines right into the cave mouth. It's a weak light, this early sunshine of the infant year, but a warming one in the lee of the rock, illumining for a while the whitened inside walls where lime water drips and spongy mosses grow.

I wish I knew more of their life and times, those shadowy ancient folk of our northern shore, but I must be content with the imagined pictures of my mind. There's a quietness about the place that provides the most pleasant of starts for my countryside calendar; a share in the accumulated peace of all the passing centuries since those folk dwelt there, living out their lives against the constant backcloth of breaking wave upon shore.

Whiskered company

FROM time to time a surfacing firth seal will view my progress along the beach with his own silent detachment. In the crystal-clear air of a year's frosty beginning, I can hear him snort and whoosh as he noses above the waves or sinks into their dark depths, taking his silent thoughts with him. In a moment he may surface surprisingly far away, seeking perhaps his chosen feeding place out in the open waters of the firth. If the whiskery snout is a large and swollen one, I know that I'm the object of attention of a big grey bull, the veteran, perhaps, of many a season among battle-scarred rivals on rocky sparring grounds where the round-eyed objects of their desires maintain a detached indifference.

I enjoy the winter presence of these sleek-coated sea mammals, for they provide cheery company on January days along the shore when the gusting north wind does its best to take your breath away. But there's a wariness, too, in the seals' company, for the hand of man is frequently raised against them, grudging them their share of the sea's largesse.

'In the bleak mid-winter . . .'

SOME winter bird habits are very predictable, and the answer to Burns's query is entirely clear as far as the starling is concerned. Each winter dusk, the farmland-foraging starlings which migrate here from the cold Baltic states and other parts of Eastern Europe flock together for their communal night-time roost.

Some of their ancestral roosting places were in sea caves, and, on the knuckle of the North-east, openings in the red granite cliffs have long attracted the birds. As dusk begins to fall, and Buchan Ness lighthouse casts its beam seawards, converging black flocks coalesce to form one excited, twittering cloud, like a gigantic bee swarm settling for a while on the roofs and aerials of nearby fisher cottages. Many a time I've marvelled at their spectacular flighting against the glow of a fiery sunset sky, before suddenly rising into the air only to drop swiftly over the cliff edge and into the cave mouth below, as if drawn into its blackness by some unseen force.

A few miles past the lighthouse and its giant foghorn companion, the bellowing 'Boddam Coo', the long-gone towering steel crane that once lifted the convict-hewn granite blocks for Peterhead's Harbour of Refuge used to house countless roosting birds. In my boyhood birdwatching days in Buchan the starling squatters flocked to the crane each winter afternoon, enjoying a lofty roosting place with a classic sea view.

Starlings are nothing if not adaptable, and town dwellers will know from experience that in winter time they've learned to make a beeline for city centres, much to the chagrin of those who prefer their office windowsills undecorated by bird droppings, and of the passers-by who daren't chance looking up, and certainly not with mouth open! The trouble is that all the elaborate flutings and cornices which adorn the grandiose city-centre buildings make ideal roosting places. In addition, the warmth from heating and lighting systems — not to mention Christmas illuminations — makes for an idyllic night-time roost, which, to a starling on a cold winter's night, must represent the next best thing to an electric blanket. Above the stir of city life below, the collective term a 'murmuration' of starlings takes on real meaning as they settle for the night. Snug in their corners above brightly-lit shops, the starlings that flock in from Eastern Europe must be grateful that the excesses of our western consumer society furnish them with such free comfort.

Nor has the prospect of a warm bed in the city passed the other birds by. Sheltered warehouses and factory roofs have long been an attraction for pied wagtails. The Invernessian wagtails which I've encountered in a multi-storey car park have opted for airy and well-lit accommodation that's definitely several stars ahead of some draughty reed bed in terms of comfort rating. Garden roosts tend to be more conventional. A dense mass of ivy on a wall or smothering an old shed provides ideal shelter. The noisy scolding of blackbirds about to bed will confirm the roosting value of dense shrubs, but the slummiest conditions of all must exist inside those garden nestboxes adopted by roosting wrens. Astounded gardeners have blinked in disbelief as up to forty tiny brown shapes have been seen departing from the entrance hole of one small box. After the night-time fug of the jampacked nest box they must surely need all the insulation they can muster in the chill air of morning.

Landscape with deer

SNOWY days bring the hill deer down to the very edges of Highland villages. Gardens are raided in the night and stock feed removed by marauding beasts driven by hunger to seek a living where they can. Journeys among the hills at this time of year become enlivened by the sight of groups of hinds or stags browsing on the lower ground, justifying the expenditure on signs exhorting drivers to beware of deer.

The population numbers of red deer in Scotland, their patterns and trends, are overseen by the Red Deer Commission. Mild winters and any reduction in culling of herds hold problems for the deer, resulting in pressure on available grazing and the inevitable conflict with farmers and crofters.

It's a noble animal, the red deer stag, carrying its antlers well, an 'Imperial' (fourteen pointer) being a prized specimen. Well-pointed antlers have always been sought after to enhance trophy collections, some of which in Victorian and later days consisted of extraordinary assemblages of mounted specimens, like the one at Mar Lodge on Royal Deeside. Hummel (hornless) stags are destined never to sport a pair of antlers at all, and are of no interest to trophy hunters.

There are few countryside experiences so memorable as the close-up sight of well-antlered stags against a winter backcloth. The whole cold scene seems to symbolise the wild nature and mood of the mountain places which the Victorian artists portrayed so powerfully.

A red deer stag stands its ground against a snowy hill backcloth. *Scotland in Focus/Ray Chaplin.*

By the winter shore

THERE can be a strange, at times almost unnerving, peacefulness about the winter shore. Though the water surface may appear calm, the aftershocks of some long-abated sea storm are registered in the mesmeric thud of the swell as it beats on the shoreline, washing the sand from the stringy roots of the marram and grinding the shingle on its downward retreat.

Oystercatchers are amongst the commonest birds of the winter shore. They frequently group together in one-legged uniformity, each long red bill deeply buried into the warmth of the pied plumage, but always with one eye firmly fixed on any potential threat, be it dog, jogger or walker. If some threat is perceived, the whole drowsy-looking bunch will shuffle seawards in a reluctant one-legged race, or rise instantly into the air, complaining noisily at the disturbance. Oystercatchers — the sea piets of the eastern coastlands — are seldom still, their fretfulness recalling the old Hebridean legend that once upon a time they were the servants of St Bride, her constant companions. But she was taken away to be the foster mother of the baby Jesus, and the oystercatchers for ever afterwards have been restless birds, always wanting to be away with her.

In a really big freeze-up, when the ground sets like iron, oystercatchers are amongst the first shore birds to suffer, their stiff black and white carcases sometimes littering the tideline. On cold nights you can hear their efforts to prise open reluctant mussel shells ringing out in the frosty air. A genuine single-shanked oystercatcher of my acquaintance was once seen dining royally on the chicken skin and Brussels sprouts throw-outs from a New Year's dinner! But for those individuals accustomed to feed by probing the soft ground of seaside fields, starvation and death may quickly follow.

As the frost sets deeper, there's a mass exodus to the coast by all sorts of birds. Woodcock, cryptically camouflaged to match the ferny woodland floor more than the patterns of open sea shore, make a last effort to find food among freezing rock pools. Among the hardened heaps of tangle, robin, redwing, blackbird and song thrush become unlikely bedfellows of turnstones and rock pipits more accustomed to such a dining place.

In a particularly vicious spell some years ago, countless redwings perished along our Black Isle shore, but their carcases didn't lie about for long, for the hoodie crows well know that in nature's scheme of things, the death of some will provide a living for others. For days afterwards, each flat-topped rock became a feather-scattered table, spread with the gory leavings of a hoodie's feast.

In a severe spell of weather the birdwatcher's best maxim may be 'expect the unexpected', even along the most familiar stretch of shore. At such times, I've encountered brent geese, normally unattracted by our coastal edge, and enjoyed the spectacle of a peregrine attempt to bring down a deftly defiant lapwing not yet prepared to become a falcon's feast. From time to time I chance upon a peregrine along our winter cliffs. Like Tennyson's eagle, clasping the crag with powerful talons, the winter falcons view the occasional human presence below with an air of supreme detachment. The female is bigger than her tiercel mate, her strongly barred plumage blending well into the craggy backcloth.

In the pink

ONE snowy New Year's Day, a friend telephoned to say that she'd chanced upon a pink gull! By this time, it was obvious that one more comment about pink elephants would be entirely unappreciated, so I went, in some disbelief, to the place where the supposed bird had been spotted. Now, the moral of this tale is clearly that in birdwatching you should never be a complete sceptic, for there, in the midst of a snow flurry, surrounded by a group of pigs whose trough was the centre of attraction, flew one decidedly pink gull. In fact, it was a black-headed gull in winter plumage, but with a rarely seen strong pink suffusion through its feathering.

Snail smasher

IN severe January days song thrushes may bang away at whelk shells on the shore in the hope of feasting on their contents. But shells of whelks are harder by far than those of the land snails which the thrushes are more adept at opening. Short of finding the actual anvil first, an insistent tapping is often the clue to a nearby snail-smashing place. The thrush's anvil may be nothing more than a sharp stone, but its effectiveness is demonstrated by the scatter of shell fragments which litter a well-used site.

The short days transform the hill hares into winter white.
Scotland in Focus/Laurie Campbell.

White hares of winter

THERE'S a loneliness about the winter uplands where the blue mountain hare makes its home, but it isn't a repelling loneliness. Rather it's one that acts as a magnet to those who love the high hills draped in snow and fashioned into fresh contours along ice cornices. There's a satisfaction in sensing the harshness of the place, yet the satisfaction is often greatest in retrospect, for these are wild places where the winter environment makes no concessions to human frailty.

The wonder is that so much life can continue there in spite of the season and its biting wind chill. The track of a hill fox across the moor, a neat pile of frozen deer droppings, the fibrous faeces of ptarmigan — nature's visiting cards are many and varied and tell of life that may be unseen but is ever-present.

The key to mountain survival is adaptation, and no hill creature is better adapted than the white hare of winter. By changing its coat to winter white and digging in to avoid the wind chill, it can make life tolerable despite the trials. It's a fine sight to see, a white winter hare bounding across the snow, protected to a degree by camouflage coat from the sharp eye of a far-seeing eagle.

On some ranges, mountain hares can be really plentiful. I suspect that geology may play a more important part in determining animal populations than we tend to think, for rock type influences vegetation, and vegetation determines food supply. On a radio programme I once heard an old gamekeeper refer to the white hares as 'Morven Jimmies' after the hill near Ballater on Deeside where they are plentiful residents. But the fine sight of white hares in winter is not for hardy hill walkers and mountain men alone, for a winter car journey over some high level road will often encounter a hare or two, though sometimes the encounter may be a fatal one as a dashing animal falls victim to fast-moving wheels.

Garden bird observatory

IN a sense, every garden is a potential observatory, where the habits and movements of birds may be monitored. At one extreme this may consist of no more than keeping an eye on the comings and goings at the bird-table; at the other it can involve maintaining an ongoing record of the birds that are present in the garden, as well as of those which pass through or over it. In the suburban setting of our first house and garden we played host to such unlikely autumn visitors as wheatear and merlin, while greenshank regularly called overhead in the spring. From our present kitchen window we take delight in the aerial displaying of buzzards, and on one memorable occasion, dishwashing was enlivened by the sight of a red kite planing along the buzzards' hill slope.

As evidence of how even a city garden can be a bird observatory, my old friend Eric Simms meticulously kept a log of all the observations which he made in his London garden over many years. From this he was able to gather much of the interesting information contained in his book *Birds of Town and Suburb*.

Keeping a note

IT'S always good to start with a new country diary as the year begins, jotting down the things which take the eye. After all, every town and city garden or park is really just a little bit of countryside in an urban setting. And in the brighter mornings and afternoons, commuter journeys can provide an opportunity for regular wildlife observation. When I used to travel a distance to work by car each day, I kept a log of different bird species seen each year, as well as an ongoing list of birds noted from the car.

And it's not just the out-of-the-ordinary that's worthy of note. Even the most everyday of happenings may form some meaningful pattern when one year is compared with the next. Commercially produced nature diaries have become popular in recent times, but at its simplest, a wildlife log may be a few brief jottings on a convenient calendar. At its finest (a state to which I've never yet aspired), it may be a complete and priceless recollection in the years to come of too easily forgotten days.

When did the first great tit burst into song? How many collared doves come down to feed? How many siskins have been at the nut bag, and what's the proportion of males to females? These are questions whose answers regularly appear in my January jottings. The enjoyment which noting them brings and the patterns which may become clear in the longer term are justification enough for keeping even the briefest of nature diary notes.

'I spy . . .'

A good pair of binoculars is a real asset, though 'good' doesn't necessarily mean some high-class, high-cost optical product. Rather it implies a suitable pair for the job. My own first binoculars hardly qualified as suitable, nor even, strictly speaking as binoculars, though through a schoolboy's eyes they were a passport to the close-up world of wildlife. They were a pair of old, brass-mounted Voigtlander field glasses brought back as booty from the German Army after the First World War! My first real binoculars were Japanese 7x50's; a bit on the heavy side, perhaps, but such an improvement with their centre-wheel focusing that I was soon able to identify the birds I'd missed before.

With such choice now available, selecting a pair of binoculars may seem a daunting task. The thing to remember is that they're classified by their makers according to magnification and the diameter of the two object lenses at the bottom end. So an 8x30 pair will magnify 8 times and let in a reasonable amount of light. An 8x40 will give the same magnification, but will be rather clearer in duller conditions since more light can enter. My own preference has always been for 8x40, but anything from 8x30 to 10x50 will do. With a higher magnification it's much more difficult to avoid the image being shaken, and the rapid beating of the heart that might accompany the first Scottish sighting of a lesser spotted something-or-other might be difficult to cope with! Some keen birdwatchers have binoculars mounted on a tripod at a window, so that the view from the garden can be surveyed at any time, but immediate access to a hand-held pair is just as good. There's nothing more infuriating than spotting something unusual and not having binoculars to tell exactly what it is.

An identification guide is absolutely essential. Any good bookshop will have a choice on offer, but after a start with *The Observer's Book of British Birds*, I grew up with *A Field Guide to the Birds of Britain and Europe* by Peterson, Mountfort and Hollom, and have gone through several copies since I began birdwatching more than three decades ago. This and some of the other field guides now available have the added advantage that they can be used when on holiday abroad, for they cover European birds as well. The Scottish Wildlife Trust, the Scottish Ornithologists' Club and the RSPB have local branches in many areas, with programmes of outings and interesting talks. Many local newspapers also have a wildlife column or diary these days, and these give good clues as to what to expect to see in the area at a particular time.

Winter in the West

A winter's day in the West may seem a dull and lifeless kind of experience compared to the bright and cheery days of summer. But it's the same landscape, only now muted by the season into more subdued tones. And the lifelessness may prove to be an illusion, as a

Round-eyed and whisker-faced, a firth seal hauls up along the shore.
Scotland in Focus/Ken Taylor.

nervous roadside grouse clatters away across the heather, or the passing of the car disturbs a heron from a roadside burn.

With the dead bracken of the past year brightened into orange-brown tones by the weak sunshine, patterns of the past are written once more on the face of the land. Beyond the green enclaves of today's croft lands, faint outlines of long-abandoned lazy beds mark peat-covered slopes like the scratchings of some giant comb. Where bracken fronds now unfurl, crofter folk once turned this grudging land with the *cas chrom* (crooked foot), the so-called foot-plough of the West, coaxing the ground into productive life with countless creels of seaware carted laboriously up from the shore. Often this was women's work, while the men worked the lines in coastal waters where shags and grey winter-plumaged tysties, the red-legged black guillemots of the north, now dive in search of squirming prey. When *buntat' 'us scadan* (tatties and herring) provided the staple diet of the folk, the shags and tysties fished in waters as yet undepleted by human greed.

Land and sea were once the people's life support, providing for their every need. Now the land provides little more than grazing for sheep and ground for growing potatoes, but here and there you may yet chance upon folk who have not completely turned their backs on the things their forebears prized. On his croft high above the waters of Loch Broom, Duncan Mackenzie of Ardindrean harvests his crop of bare-branched willow on January days when the whistling of wigeon drakes rises from below. Then, in the dark evenings after croft work is done, he weaves the supple stems from burnside willows into the strong baskets which country folk once employed; the skills of the past living on in today's countryside.

FEBRUARY

'The mavis, doon thy bughted glade,
Gars echo ring frae ev'ry tree.'

ROBERT TANNAHILL

*F*EBRUARY is winter's real make-or-break month; a chance to assert itself before March follows with all its unstoppable signs of spring's approach. This unpredictability of character is closely tied to the battle of the air flows with their differing source regions. When the air comes blasting down from the Arctic north, dampened by its ocean journeying, the month may be dour and dismal. But when a southerly stream brings Saharan desert air with it, things may take on an altogether more promising look. At its best, February may then unfold as a gentle month of green-ruffed yellow aconites and white snowdrop drifts, and of that first excited calling of the oystercatchers over the farmlands.

A bird by any other voice

THE lengthening days act as a great spur to the countryside's early singers. The slightest blink of sun sends the chimney pot starlings into raptures of scratchy song, their inherited passages often jumbled up with sounds remembered from other days. In this way, I've been fooled into looking up at a non-existent passing curlew, and into putting my binoculars on to the hillside to search for mewing buzzards that were never there. Nor have the ventriloquist acts stopped at that. Over the years, a succession of starling virtuosos have given us the odd barking dog, puling herring gull and crowing cock, just to liven things up a bit.

I feel really lifted by an outpouring of February starling song. Whenever I see an enthusiastic bird throwing out his throat feathers and launching into his scratchy serenade, I think of a little valley farm

16

Drifts of white snowdrops bring promise of better days to come.
Scotland in Focus/Laurie Campbell.

I know in Norway where the farmer puts up nestboxes to welcome back the birds, because, to the valley folk, the starling's coming symbolises winter's going. But I recall also my blinking disbelief when he said that he'd ejected a rare wryneck from one of the boxes because it was taking up a potential starling nesting place!

Gang laigh hens

EVEN our little black bantam cock seems disposed at this time to join the early singers with neck-stretched gusto. Though he's a fluffy, feathery-footed Pekin, descendant of some live booty taken from the sacking of the palace in Peking last century, we felt he should have a Scottish name, so 'Cock of the North' he became, proud protector of his little harem. Much as I like the Pekins, I must confess to missing our late-lamented Scots Dumpies. Scotland can claim two native poultry breeds, the one a gamey bird with immaculately barred plumage and fine flowing tail called the Scots Grey and the other its decidedly more down-to-earth cousin, the Dumpy. Once known as 'gang laighs' for their low-slung carriage which gives them a duck's waddle, Dumpies have the shortest shanks imaginable. Their stronghold used to be the West Coast, but over the years they were eclipsed by more utility fowls.

The Dumpy is one of the success stories in domestic livestock conservation, having teetered on the brink of extinction till help was at hand in the form of some birds imported from Africa, the descendants of stock which had gone out there with a Scots lady decades before. They must have thrived in the African air, which is more than can be said for the Dumpies which years ago were sent to an estate south of the Border. Far from their native soil, the birds moped and moulted, apparently pining for the north. Then one day a Highland gamekeeper employed on the estate happened to pass their coop and absent-mindedly gave the dejected birds a Gaelic greeting. At once the Dumpies perked up, and with a regular dose of the native tongue they were soon on the way to red-combed, egg-laying glory again. . . . Well, it's a good story, anyway!

Where wild goats graze

THERE'S a fine big cave beneath the craggy slopes of Craigiehowe overlooking the Inverness Firth. An old Black Isle man, born and brought up not many miles away, once told me how families of tinks used to be drawn each summer to the cave, to live and work there for the season. He recalled their expertise in metal working, for they were travelling folk of the old order, craftsmen who tinkered in tin and other metals. Heather besoms, their wiry stems tightly wrapped round a straight trimmed branch, were another speciality.

The tinks have long gone, but their cave home is occupied yet, albeit on an intermittent basis. At times it forms a refuge for a tribe of wild goats which graze among the heather and blasted pines above. Even when the cave is empty, you're left in no doubt that the goats have been around, for all the perfumes of Arabia would be gey sorely pressed to counter the aroma of a well-seasoned old billy.

Their forebears supplied a little milk for the crofters who once eked a living from the thin ground of the adjacent hillsides. The folk have long gone from the place and the old croft houses lie deserted and eyeless with their empty windows, but the goats have stayed on, in varying mixtures of colour from white to black and all the piebald patterning in between.

Surprisingly, perhaps, this early part of the year is the time of the wild goats' kidding throughout the Scottish countryside. Weather, fox and eagle all take their toll, for it's a testing time to come into the world in such wild settings, but one of my favourite of all late winter sights is that of tiny kids playing round the staid nannies as their billygoat father with flowing beard and scimitar horns looks impassively on.

There are many fine surviving goat tribes still, despite the depredations of foreign trophy hunters and the elimination of others in the interest of young forest plantations. Wild goats are no strangers to hill walkers in many places. I've enjoyed them as a complement to the red deer on the fine mountain lands of Kintail at one end of the land, and they roam the sweeping hill slopes around Clatteringshaws in the Galloway Forest Park at the other. Hardy winter walkers along the West Highland Way may glimpse a young goat or two also as they pass on their way.

In recent times, some feral goats have been removed to a life of captivity to be cross-bred with exotic Angoras to put some Scots smeddum into the fibre-producing flocks. They're nothing if not hardy, these living relics from the old crofting days. Once, it was apparently no uncommon sight to see a goat cropping the green growth that sprouted among thatched cottage roofs. But the classic wild goat country to my mind is one of fallen rock and tumbled scree, like the bleak slopes of Slocht Summit on the A9 where I always look out for their well-camouflaged forms as I pass beneath them on the road. In that wild Highland setting the wiry-haired goats lead their playful kids to browse among ancient junipers that are gnarled and bleached by the blasting wind and stinging sleet of countless hard winters.

Robins in a rage

THE cock robin, too, now expresses his *joie de vivre* in spring song, exchanging the melancholy cadences of winter in the garden for spirited song passages designed to woo a female partner. All this must throw the local robin establishment into quite a tizzy, for both cock and hen birds have been putting up a vigorous defence of their own territories since the autumn days. It was the poet Blake who said that the sight of a robin in a cage put all Heaven in a rage, but robins are more than capable of working up their own wrath. Like a red rag to a bull, red feathers to a robin are a signal to attack. Only where there's food or water available are the barriers lowered for the necessities of life to be attended to.

So, belligerent cock robins must adjust to the urge to entice a suitable female redbreast into what has until now been a sacrosanct patch. Excessive male chauvinism must now be overcome, and there's the rub, for nature has conditioned the robin to regard any other red-breasted individual as an interloper. In the end, though, all is sorted out, in the interests of ensuring a new generation when the better days come, but, while it lasts, what a tangled web the robins weave in resolving their love-hate complexes.

The wee cock sparra

HOUSE sparrows, too, those underrated residents of town and city streets, are coaxed into pair formation at this time. Belonging to the weaver family of birds which produce such neatly woven nests in other parts of the world, our spurgie or speug seems destined never to master the art. Its untidy nests can be seen stuffed into any suitable nook or cranny, serving also as a roost throughout the winter.

Like the cock robin, an unmated cock sparrow now finds himself in a bit of a dilemma. Wanting to attract a mate, he chirrups as loudly as he can beside his nest hole and shivers his wings suggestively at any passing female, but the urge to fend off any intruder remains. So, just like the female robin, the sparrow's potential mate must be persistent and prepared to put up with a dreadful show of manners if she's to be accepted.

Common though it is in its favoured urban environment, the sparrow isn't the nation's most numerous bird. That distinction goes to the chaffinch, though in the winter months the vast immigrant flocks may considerably boost the starling's total. Nor, I suspect, is the sparrow always the best known of garden birds, despite years of close cohabitation with man. Yet, in the nation's cultural heritage, it has found its own fame, for who could ever forget the late Duncan MacRae's immortal rendering of the 'Wee Cock Sparra' which, perhaps in the expectation of enticing a mate, sat 'chirpin' awa' on the shafts o' the barra'.

The well-spotted song thrush, most powerful of the countryside's early singers.
Scotland in Focus/Eric Middleton.

The wise thrush

PERHAPS of all February's new songs, the most welcome is that of the
song thrush, the 'mavis wild, wi' mony a note', as Burns described it,
and other poets have waxed eloquent on the subject of this lovely
singer. Wordsworth was taken with the sheer power of the bird
singing 'At the corner of Wood Street when daylight appears', and
Browning was struck with the repetition and insistence of the bird's
song passages when he wrote:

> *'That's the wise thrush; he sings each song twice over,*
> *Lest you should think he never could recapture*
> *The first fine careless rapture.'*

Early mornings and dusk are best for appreciating the thrush's fresh
song in days when all that the blackbird can manage is a subdued
practice of better things to come. Countless dreich mornings have
been made the cheerier for me on my way to work through hearing a
neighbourhood mavis in full February flow.

Ducks of the winter shore

ALONG the edge of our winter firth there's usually a fair scattering of sea ducks. Mallard appear only when ice freezes their preferred inland pools, but the maritime red-breasted mergansers pursue their coordinated fishing close to shore. They remind me of pictures of native fishermen wading in some African river, arranged in a circle as they cast their nets upon the surrounded shoals. When in groups mergansers often work that way, heads underwater as they swim towards a central point, driving any fish before them.

From time to time a diving bird will surface with some hopelessly complicated crustacean that defies easy swallowing. Twisting and turning it this way and that in its serrated red bill, the merganser eventually arrives at a solution, and down the legs and arms go, waving and wriggling their protest as they disappear from view. Then, with a final flourish, the happy hunter shakes itself and attends to a quick preen of ruffled neck feathers.

Goldeneye also have their favourite stretches of shore which draw them year after year. Often it's the smart drakes that frequent our nearby shallow waters, their broad heads and prominent white eye spots setting them apart from all the other ducks of the winter shore. Perhaps a few of these are now Scottish-bred birds rather than Scandinavian immigrants, for goldeneye have taken to nestboxes in trees alongside Highland lochs, their fluffy youngsters tumbling out from nest holes in trees that are high above the ground.

In the eastern firths, long-tailed ducks are often the sea ducks *par excellence* of February days. They usually perform their mad dashings and splashings far from shore, but their strange haunting calls carry far across the water. 'Coal an' can'le licht' was what east-coast folk thought the ducks were calling out, and Peter Cunningham in his book *A Hebridean Naturalist* refers to a tradition from Berneray in Harris of the birds being called McCandlay-eun, McCandlay's bird, because of the supposed similarity of the call to the old island surname of McCandlay.

Long-tailed ducks really are classic winter birds. The smart appearance of the drake with his brown and cream plumage and jaunty long tail is strongly reinforced in the appearance in all-male groups, sometimes forty or more at a time, as they fast-flight close to shore. On clear February mornings, their clangorous calling fairly

Still days of winter reflect the subdued colouring of the goldeneye duck.
Scotland in Focus/Laurie Campbell.

echoes along the firthlands. I like to stand by the lapping shore in the atmospheric setting of morning as the rising sun sharpens the dark outlines of the distant Monadhliath, listening to the wild chorus of the long-tails and the eerie cries of red-throated divers piercing the still air as they flight in from the open sea.

'Lark song and sea sounds'

FOR some reason, song thrushes give our garden a miss during the winter, but make a welcome reappearance in February days. Skylarks also, absent for weeks on end, suddenly reappear in the seaside fields, trilling and circling about as though pleased to be back. By the time the month is nearing its end, the first brave attempts at new song are filtering down from a few first soaring birds, a bit uncertainly at first, perhaps, but soon developing into a full song to thrill the March days to come.

Our favourite local skylark gathering ground is the seaside golf course, and on a fine February day when the sun shines and a gentle swell is lapping the shore, I'm reminded of John Betjeman's experience of another links golf course with

> 'Lark song and sea sounds in the air
> And splendour, splendour everywhere.'

Promise of spring

NOT all our countryside plants are long-entrenched natives. The alien white butterbur has successfully spread throughout eastern Scotland, its green rhubarb-like leaves gracing many a lowland verge and burnside. Yet long before the foliage even starts to unfurl, the white clustered flowers are already providing a seasonal uplift in the dark days of winter. Like aconite and snowdrop, butterbur is a plant that's far from dormant at the dead end of the year. In fact, its early budding is one of nature's real promises of spring, and for that reason well worth seeking. I make an annual pilgrimage to look for them along a seaside water flow on dark February days when there's little else of cheer around. With only the tripping of the burn and the distant trilling of a dipper for company, the butterbur's fat bursting buds mark the cold bareness of the ground with countless eruptions that express their urge to open to the lengthening light.

Mysterious scarts

THERE'S no telling what the cormorants of our firth think of the long-tails' wild cavortings around them, for they pass the time impassively on the red-painted navigation buoys that mark out the deep water channel, whiles craning their necks at the goings-on around them, whiles hanging out their wings to dry and give the appearance of the fossil *archaeopterix*. Their guttural chatter sometimes drifts across to shore, but they keep themselves to themselves, vacating their roosting buoys only for the men on the lighthouse tender who have the

A cormorant in heraldic pose hangs its wings in the sea breeze.
Scotland in Focus/Laurie Campbell.

unsavoury task of removing their fishy guano. Once, northern folk were content to eat these birds, first burying their carcases in the ground to rid the flesh of its fishy taint.

On the Black Isle coast there's a cliff called the Scarts Craig where the cormorants, or scarts, gather in the gloaming, their primitive black shapes outlined for a moment against the fading sky before settling to land. Streams of fishy droppings whiten the cliff-face and have long since killed all life in the tree branches to which their great web-feet somehow manage to cling. I always think of cormorants as birds of mystery, an impression guaranteed to be heightened by a late afternoon visit to their dank-smelling roosting place.

'Merry dancers in the sky'

WHEN February skies clear to a starry deepness, we're sometimes treated to a display of the Northern Lights. *Aurora borealis*, the Merry Dancers; small wonder folk thought of them in that way, for the multitude of patterned shafts and rays fairly dance across the sky. In recent times we've had some exceptional displays, auguring well for the years to come, for scientists predict that we're in for some fine entertainment on winter nights. Once, folk thought they were seeing the light bouncing off the polar ice caps, but in our age of scientific enlightenment we take the physicists' word for it that the Merry Dancers are the result of atomic particles in the solar wind being drawn polewards to Earth.

A good-going display of the Aurora is at once an impressive and an eerie experience. Starry nights are frequently still nights as well, and you half expect to hear some sound as the lights bounce across the sky above, and weave back and fore like the opening and closing of a heavenly curtain. Small wonder folk once believed they could actually hear the gentle swish of the pink and green-tinged curtains in the sky. Analogies change with the generations' experience, and one recent display was described to me as looking 'like disco lights', a fitting description of a night when the whole sky above seemed to quiver in constant colourful change. Yet, however much we may have learned from the scientists' study of this strange phenomenon, nothing can take away the sheer wonder of it all as the Northern Lights dance their merry way across the night sky.

After the ice

IN many ways, the face of our Scottish countryside can be read like a
textbook on glaciation, and winter days serve to highlight the text.
The landscape was moulded by the passage of ice, for it was glaciers
and frost shattering together that fretted the sides of history-steeped
Glencoe and fashioned our wide straths. The strange Parallel Roads
of Glen Roy mark the successive levels of an emptying loch that was
dammed up by ice, and the ice-gouged, deep defile of the Lairig Ghru
has successively played the role of drover's pass and hill-walker's link
between Strathspey and Deeside. Close by, the whole of Speyside's
skiing industry exists by virtue of the fact that the facing Cairngorms
massif is scalloped by the glacier-scoured bowls of Coire na Ciste and
Coire Cas, now draped with all the ironmongery that accompanies
such developments in mountain places everywhere.

But the after-effects of the Ice Age aren't seen only in a Highland
context. The 'basket of eggs' topography of the South-west is created
by ovoid swells of boulder clay deposited by the ice sheet, allowing
Scotland's City of Culture to boast some analogy with Rome as being a
city built on hills. Edinburgh's Royal Mile sweeps down from the
Castle by virtue of being the tail end of a classic crag and tail
formation formed when moving ice met the resistant volcanic plug of
the Castle Rock.

Colonel F. Rainsford-Hannay has written eloquently of the
drystane dykes of Galloway, fashioned from ice-scattered boulders and
with their own colourful dykers' terms, such as clonks and lunky
holes. The old stone walls have become monuments to their makers,
men such as Davie the Dyker in John McTaggart of Borgue's poem
early last century who clearly was a master craftsman, content with
nothing but his best:

> *'A rickled rood ne'er left his han',*
> *His dykes for centuries will stan'...'*

(A rood is the length of a day's dyking work).

In the lowland North-east, the lines of the farmlands are drawn in the
straight field edges of drystane dykes laboriously constructed from
boulders bequeathed by the wasted ice. Around Monymusk and

Kingswells in Aberdeenshire they're so wide that they're known as 'consumption dykes' because they consumed so many of the stones off the fields. At times they're broad enough to have a good-sized path run along them (the giant Kingswells dyke being twenty-seven feet across its flat top). I taught some country pupils in a nearby school who travelled each day in the manner of their forebears, following on foot the straight lines of farm dykes raised up with the stones the ice left behind.

In so many respects, the effects of the ice are writ so large upon the face of our countryside that when next complaining of February's dreichness, we would do well to ponder on what a real Scottish winter must once have been like!

Moulded by ice, the U-shaped valley of Loch Broom provides a fine setting for Highland cattle. *Douglas Willis*.

MARCH

'My bonnie tatties lookit braw
Till three coorse deils cam ben the raw,
Frost and mowdiewarp and craw.'

J. C. MILNE

*T*HE merest hint of warmth in a shaft of March sunshine is
enough to boost the business of our village hardware store.
Winter bird food is now set aside as temperatures start to rise,
and bags of seed potatoes and racks of colourful flower seed packets
are displayed to tempt the eye. Investing in a new season's seeds at
this time becomes almost a symbolic act, a hopeful passport to the
better days to come. But it may all be a trap for the unwary gardener,
for piercing night frosts which may follow the daytime opening of
crocus flowers will nip incipient tattie sprouts and harden the dark
earth heaps where unseen mowdiewarps criss-cross the fields with the
spoil from their underground molings.

Mad March hares

IN country lore, March is the time for mad hares. The ones which
sometimes launch themselves in front of my car are perhaps more
foolhardy than feeble-minded, but living as I do in a countryside
where rabbits are two-a-penny, it comes as a pleasant change to see
the lang-luggit outline of a hare bounding across the bare parks. In
fact, the hares' strange boxing is nothing more than pure male show-
off to impress the females at the start of the mating season.

Not far from our house, courting partridges share the same
stubble fields as the sparring March hares, but the interest of the
pairtricks is more in sealing their own seasonal bond, with all the
creaky utterings which that entails.

Life at the top

BY now, the late afternoon ritual of rooks and jackdaws flighting to winter roosts has been abandoned in the interests of rearing a new generation. We tend to take rooks fairly much for granted, but what better way for the birdwatcher to celebrate the earliest days of spring than to stand and watch the ongoings at a rookery.

My own favourite March rookery is a modest affair in the canopy of some old seaside pines, where the glossy black occupants caw against a background of lapping tide on the beach below. As the eruptions of sandy moleheaps increase beneath the pines, the rooks are busy settling into their time-honoured, noisy nesting routine, and all the preliminaries of bowing and scraping give way to serious courtship ritual as incubation of the spotty green eggs begins. Stylised it may be, but the love play of the rooks is still a touching performance to observe, as they affirm their raucous relationships.

Standing beneath the bedlam of a rookery on a fresh March day is one of those experiences which can really lift the spirit and confirm the coming of better times. The wind may whistle through the leafless branches, but for the nesting crows life at the top proceeds undaunted. Sometimes there's a sudden rain of twigs as somebody fails to solve a tricky construction problem up aloft, and there's nothing like a sleekit bit of stick-pinching when a neighbour's back is turned, just to add to the rumpus!

Rookery watching needn't be for country dwellers only, for the rook clan has many town septs. Kirkwall in largely treeless Orkney manages its town colony, and on windswept Lewis the island capital has its complement, too, in the Stornoway woods. In student days in Aberdeen, I really appreciated the March ongoings at the rookery in Union Terrace Gardens, that priceless oasis of green in the heart of the city's granite greyness. In the most depressing of days, when sleet showers whirled among the shoppers and the place took on its dourest of moods, the city-centre rooks were an unfailingly cheery presence, their nests separated only by a few feet from the tops of the cream and green double-decker buses below.

And the rooks remain defiantly there yet, despite threats of eviction in a plan to redevelop this part of the city centre. But for now, the city-centre rookery is definitely a case of *rus in urbe*, or to

Starkly outlined rookeries resound to their cawing spring chorus.
Scotland in Focus/Laurie Campbell.

put it into less classical North-east terms, the kintra-side in 'e toon.

Kirkyards are favourite rookery places, their cawing choruses a cheering reminder of the renewal of life in a setting preoccupied with its ending. The isolated community of rooks in Ullapool, a village not short of choice of religious denominations, appear at first sight to have opted for the established kirk, since they build their nests exclusively outside the Church of Scotland and in the trees down the road at its manse. Of course, it all has more to do with the supply of suitable nesting trees than with any preference for one religious persuasion over another, but in their shiny black suits the Ullapool rooks are certainly impeccably dressed for the Sabbath!

Strangers from afar

TOWN life clearly has some appeal for the rook. The collared dove's commitment is more firm, for there can scarcely be town or village the length and breadth of Scotland that doesn't now have its complement of these pale fawn doves with characteristic black neck ring, cooing from the rooftops. It's difficult now to think of collared doves as immigrants, yet, as a boy, I recall birdwatchers being fired by the sensational news that a completely new bird had started to colonise the country in the late 1950s, after a dramatic spread from drier lands to the east.

By chance, one of the first sites to be occupied in Britain was beside Lossiemouth on the Moray Firth. With collared doves now practically everywhere, it's strange also to think that I actually persuaded my parents to take me all the way over from Aberdeenshire to see those first Scottish collared doves among the trees at Covesea Farm. It's changed days now, for the bird's spread has taken it as far west as it can go, short of an Atlantic crossing, and the collared dove has embraced its Scottish nationality with a total enthusiasm.

It was the coo-COO-coo calling from rooftop and television aerial that first alerted folk to the arrival of strangers in their midst, and many were the reports of unseasonable cuckoos. From a personal point of view, I had cause to be grateful for the confusion, for, as an aspiring schoolboy writer, it provided me with a topical subject for my very first country diary note in the 'Buchanie', the affectionate local name for the Buchan Observer.

Again like the rooks, collared doves are happy enough to construct their nests among bare branches at this time of year, but they make such a poor job of the twiggy platforms that you can easily see the white eggs right through the flimsy bottom. In fact, the doves have a prolonged nesting season which partly explains the speed of their colonisation. Occasionally, a few much paler individuals turn up in the big gatherings which forage around country villages, and for a time we had one in the garden which was pure white, apart from some fawn markings along its tail.

Riddle of the rocks

BARE rock faces are hardly in short supply in the far North-west, but by the side of the main road on Inverpolly National Nature Reserve there's a particular rocky outcrop which once set the geological establishment into a real tizzy. Knockan Cliff near Lochinver, with its sheer variety of rock formations, is a place to stop and ponder our land's geological origins, for its story is unfolded in an interpretative display and along a nature trail.

The normal and logical sequence of rocks is to have the oldest at the bottom and the younger ones successively above them, ending with the most recent closest to the surface. But at Knockan things are far from being that simple, for ancient Moine Schists lie on top of much younger rock. So what can have happened to defy nature's rules?

Along an important divide known to geologists as the Moine Thrust Plane, older rocks were heaved bodily westwards to confound the experts of Victorian days who first wrestled with the problem of why older rocks could possibly lie above much younger formations. All this is believed to have happened during the Caledonian mountain-building period some 400 million years ago. The result is that Knockan Cliff is of outstanding international importance as a classic geological site, providing clues to the interpretation of mountain landscapes everywhere.

I like to visit Knockan best at this winter time when things are quiet; when the yellow spreads of mountain saxifrage are but a summer memory and the lonely calling of greenshanks across the peat flows only an imagined echo from warmer days. The peat-stained lochs are rippled now by gusting wind rather than by surfacing diver, but it's then that the mind is concentrated wonderfully on the bare bones of our landscape.

Of all Knockan's interesting rock formations my favourite is the pipe rock whose strange fossil markings have preserved for all time the briefest burrowings of humble marine sandworms, providing a reminder of the earliest forms of life in the area.

For the interested amateur too, a stone wall on Knockan Cliff places the various rocks into their correct sequence in the geological past. Below the grey Moine Schists with their sparkling mica at the top of the wall sits the Durness Limestone, best known for its wonderful cave formation at Smoo further still to the north. But not quite so far removed, in the vicinity of Inchnadamph, lie some lesser-known caverns from which the bones of Arctic reindeer, lemming and bear have been identified, and which once afforded shelter for earliest man. But my oddest experience with the Inchnadamph caves concerned the finding one day not of Arctic animal bones but of a half-consumed candle, an unoccupied pair of wellies and, most intriguing of all, a copy of the latest edition of *Punch*!

Songs of spring

'WHERE are the songs of spring?' enquired the poet. Well, on a fine March morning they're certainly given a fresh airing, for now the dawn chorus really starts to grow, and it's good to be able to lie in bed and identify its separate strands. The monotonous cooing of collared dove and unrestrained bellowing of herring gull may be less lovely parts in the swelling chorus than those of blackbird, song thrush, dunnock and great tit, but it's the sheer power in the daily upturn of volume that impresses on a dark March morning, never mind for now the need to shut the window to turn it down when the chorus reaches a crescendo in the earlier dawns of April and May.

On the whin-covered slope beside our house, the first yellow-hammer song now takes its place once more in the sound backcloth. Most bird books will say that the yellowhammer sings 'A little bit of bread and no chee-eese!' but no self-respecting Scots yalla yites could surely give voice to such Anglicised utterings. What they really shout out is the much more forthright 'Deil, deil, tak yee-ee!'

Stirrings in the kirk

MARCH sunshine — however brief — brings its special rewards, like the sight of the first honey bee at an open crocus flower, the sacs on its thighs tightly packed with bright orange pollen, or the first tortoiseshell butterfly fluttering at the window of a garden shed.

Sometimes we see an early tortoiseshell take a bit flutter round the pews in the village kirk on a March Sunday morning, but the same faint warmth filtering through the stained glass seems to send the early bluebottles into a complete frenzy, buzzing furiously round the heads of the congregation in daredevil passes that make you itch to take an unseemly swipe at them as they pass.

Of course, such ongoings are calculated to transport your mind far away from the minister's sermon, but when my conscience is troubled by such diversions into the realms of natural history, I take a certain consolation in recalling that there's a good Scots precedent for wildlife watching in the kirk. If Burns hadn't been similarly preoccupied with studying a beastie's progress across the lady's hat in the pew in front, the world might have been deprived of those oft-quoted lines in 'To a Louse':

> *'O wad some Power the giftie gie us,*
> *To see oursels as ithers see us!'*

'The flowers that bloom in the spring . . .'

THE ways of nature may seem familiar and predictable, but the truth is that there's infinite variety in the apparently familiar pattern. On mild March days, just note how the first stirrings of spring come a little earlier to south-facing slopes.

On crisp March mornings I sometimes flush a woodcock from his secret feeding place on a damp, sunbathed bank above our nearby stretch of disused railway line. It's in such favoured spots that the first primrose and celandine are stirred into welcome opening, pushing in their enthusiasm through the fallen leaves of the past year. Though we may take it for granted, it's no accident that the flowers that bloom early in spring share the same colour. In the March countryside it's

In garden and public park, the golden-throated crocus is the bright
harbinger of spring. *Scotland in Focus/Roger Fox.*

the bright blossom that catches the early bee, and yellow seems to be
just the right shade for the job.

With our neighbourhood buzzards mewing and wheeling in
display above the bare tree tops, I'm reminded that it's time to look for
early frogspawn along pond margins and round the rims of lochs. The
water may still seem uninviting to human touch, but the puddock's
calendar is regulated in ways that are meaningless to us.

A bird by any other name . . .

HOW cheering to generations of farm folk was the lapwing's return as
the dark days of winter rolled by. Lapwing, teuchat, peewit, peesie,
peesieweep; the name may have differed, but the bird's reappearance
had the same meaning — the slackening of winter's grip on the
country places.

Flora Garry weaves that evocative cry of tentative spring days into her poem 'The Quine an the Teuchats', as the peewits rise in twinkling flight over new-sown farm parks:

> *'An wallochy-wallochy-weet the teuchats rise*
> *Ower the new-shauven leys'.*

This animated display is a preliminary to the aerobatics and courtship calling that once filled the farmlands and permeated the writing of the folk who knew both them and the birds well, perhaps no more so than in Lewis Grassic Gibbon's *Sunset Song*.

Like 'peewit', 'teuchat' is a name probably derived from the bird's calling, but a country loon in a North-east school asked me one day, 'Please sir, is that bird ca'd a teuchat 'cause it's teugh tae ate?' Unfortunately, never having eaten one, I was unable to comment on the toughness or otherwise of its texture!

In green sheen and sleek crest, was there ever such a fine symbol of Scotland's spring countryside? Now the face of our farmlands bears the marks of a machine-dominated age. In his draughtproof cabin,

The smartly-plumaged lapwing brings life and sound to the awakening countryside. *Scotland in Focus/Laurie Campbell.*

shielded from engine noise by ear-muffs or canned music, today's farmer is more insulated from the cold and isolated from the sounds of the countryside. Not so the old-time ploughman who followed the furrows behind his pair of horse to the accompaniment of the teuchats' spring symphony, stopping whiles to carry a clutch of bonny pointed eggs in the warmth of his bonnet to some safer place removed from the horses' trampling feet. How sad to think that once this was a hated bird in parts of Southern Scotland, its agitated calling a betrayal of the Covenanters out on the lonely moors.

If the 'gyaun aboot' hens that scratched a living round the farmyard's midden heap happened to be off the lay, there was a temptation to view the teuchats' eggs as a seasonal country harvest, but the birds were allowed to get on with the job of laying a fresh clutch, and little harm was probably done. In fact, there may sometimes even have been an advantage in it for the birds, since March clutches were at the mercy of the bitter wintry weather which might settle back among the farmlands on any day, bringing 'teuchat storms' as reminder of the month's fickleness of mood.

That March is an uncertain interlude between the winter grip of February and April's spring growth is sometimes all too obvious, as late snows bring 'lambing storms' to attend the birthpangs of restless early ewes, and sometimes hap them in drifts behind stone dykes.

Gentle giants

OF the heavy horses which once worked the land in the days of the teuchat, there are plenty reminders still. The disused chaumers or bothies of the ploughmen survive here and there, dotted about the lowland farmscape. But the stone and wood cartsheds of the old farm steadings, fashioned for the horse carts of the time, now suffer all the bumps and knocks of their changed fortunes, for they're not of this farming age, and great combines can't be manoeuvred in a confined space like a well-trained 'Jock' or 'Bess'.

Clydesdale horses, for long the hard-working gentle giants of the Scottish farming scene. *Scotland in Focus/Ray Chaplin.*

Of the gentle giants themselves, memories abound in town and countryside alike. The clatter of metal-shod hooves over granite cassies rings through my mind yet as I recall pairs of great beasts, loused from their labours around the fish yards and kippering kilns of the 'Blue Toon', following at the trot behind a horseman as he biked his way towards the wee 'parkies' dotted around the town. There, freed from their daytime toil, they happily chomped their way through the night.

But in the face of all the change, Scotland's own great horse, the Clydesdale, refuses to be consigned to the past. A pair or two still put in a well-rehearsed appearance at some of the spring ploughing matches, but I was jolted out of my torpor on a train journey one day by a completely unrehearsed performance that's lingered in my mind. In the fields at the Heavy Horse Centre between Perth and Dundee, half a dozen great Clydesdales were unashamedly prancing one after another in the March sunshine, manes flowing and great legs kicking out behind as if they were fresh spring foals.

I can't help feeling that it's somehow good for the soul to be in the company of such fine beasts every now and again, which is why I head each year for Aberdeen's Duthie Park to marvel once more at the grace and beauty of whole lines of these gentle Scottish giants at the popular Clydesdale Show.

The wild West

ACROSS in the crofting West, where hard frosts and blizzards are less troublesome to the folk who wrest a living from the land, March may still deal a stinging card, as one wild day in Assynt made me all too aware. Motoring north past Loch Broom, there were already omens of the day to come, for the klondyker ships with their tattered hammer and sickle flags were beginning to strain at their moorings like restless beasts.

Further to the north, the towering forms of Canisp and Suilven stood solidly aloof, but beyond the lochside ruins of Ardvreck Castle, the gale was piling white foam high against the far bank. Few birds dared remain airborne. Only a solitary buzzard braved the blast, a long stick tightly grasped in his talons. Fighting to retain some control, he sailed away across the treeless land, still clutching his dangling prize.

At the side of the loch I tried to open the door of the car, but the wind was firmly set against it. Now the blast was forcing life once more into the dead bracken fronds, tumbling them crazily along the road, and for a moment I wondered whether the rocking car would join them. In the lee of a pine-covered islet, a courting couple of mallard sheltered as best they could. Agitated by my presence, they were reluctant to commit themselves to the fury of thr storm. At last their nerve broke, and they rose into the buffeting, tossed first this way then the other, before finally returning to the loch surface again in an undignified crash-landing.

By next morning, the wind had dropped, and the klondykers were barely moving, their rusty hulks reflecting in the stillness of the loch. Such an unpredictable month is March, occupant of the country calendar slot between all the uncertainty of a Scottish winter and the promised days of spring.

APRIL

'There's burstin buds on the larick now,
A the birds are paired an' biggin'...'

CHARLES MURRAY

*A*PRIL days bring rapid change to our country places, giving encouragement to the vibrant growth of spring. At their best they are days of unfolding softness, yet days, too, when the numbing cold of winter can wait with menace in the wings, sending a last chill blast to slow for a while the season's quickening pulse.

West Coast days

MOST visitors' experience of the West Coast is in summer days, but the days around Easter have an attraction that is no less strong. Small herds of whooper swans sometimes rest a while from their northwards journeying on the placid waters of lochs brimful with snow melt, and driving becomes the more enjoyable for seeing their white forms ripple the inverted hill images. On the surrounding bleak brown moors, sharp-eyed grey and black hoodie crows scan for signs of death, for winter on the open hill is a test that only the fittest are permitted to pass, and nature's sharp-eyed undertakers are always on call.

Beneath the snowcapped hills the red deer often gather close to roadsides, viewing the passing cars with cool detachment. How strange to think that these creatures of the open hill were once forest dwellers. Now their numbers have soared, and a nocturnal encounter with a deer along a Highland roadside is commonplace.

Further to the west, the Atlantic ends of the country enjoy more kindly influences. Along this western fringe the North Atlantic Drift bathes the coastline with a last warm trace of the Gulf Stream. The milder air keeps at bay the frosts which catch out the frogs on the hill lochans, and few sights are more miserable than that of frosted puddocks' eggs on a chill April day! The fishing village of Ullapool can boast a veteran palm tree or two on the strength of it, and in the sheltered garden of Inverewe, by the shores of deep Loch Ewe, brightening cock chaffinches cheer the April days with freshly practised song among exotic growth. Osgood Mackenzie's vision of a verdant oasis on that bleak western peninsula now finds satisfying fulfilment among rhododendron thickets rarely troubled by the stinging frosts which lay hold of the nearby hills.

The loch isle of Innis Maree

THESE are quiet times along West Coast roads. Days may be shorter than in summer, but with the new season's tourist flow scarcely started, there's time to stand and stare without a whole lot of passing cars stopping to see what it is you're staring at! In all of the Highlands, there are few prospects so splendid as the view down to Loch Maree. On the loch itself, a scatter of wooded islands enhances an already rich landscape. But while most of the loch islands are clothed in ancient pines, there's another smaller and mystic little isle that's draped in its own tangled spread of larch, oak and holly.

Innis Maree isn't the largest of the loch islands, but in historical terms it's by far the richest. Even Queen Victoria couldn't resist its charms on her visit to sample the grandeur of the area.

One brisk April morning, with white-capped Slioch as backcloth to the blue ribbon of the loch, the boatman ferried me out from Talladale in his brown-varnished clinker boat. We made short work of the crossing, passing a solitary black-throated diver on the water and a smart drake goldeneye fast-flighting down the loch, the sound of his rapid wing beats singing in the clear air.

Above the gravelly shores of the little island, nothing stirred but a single robin who viewed this intrusion into his quiet world with ill-concealed curiosity. Steeped in ancient lore, Isle Maree is a holy place where the saintly Maelrubha built his cell. Once, there was a sacred water issue here, a clootie well, where rags were tied to a nearby oak. In course of time, offerings of money were made by hammering pennies and halfpennies sideways into the trunk. Though the tree has long since died of copper poisoning, its remains survive, thickly studded in coins greened with age, from a distance looking like the scaly limbs of some prehistoric monster.

Gathering geese and fishy fowl

ALONG the eastern lowlands it's a time for seeing the movements of gathering geese. April's lengthening days bring unrest to flocks that have foraged the winter long among the farmlands. Wavering skeins of high-pitched pinkfeet and of more nasal-sounding greylags traverse the country, on the first stage of their northward haul. Their excited calling is a feature of the month, echoing over farmland and town alike, as they pass in great waves. Silhouetted against the sky, exact identification may be difficult, but on the ground dark heads distinguish the pinkfeet from the greylags with their paler plumage and bright orange bills.

Scanning the goose flocks for strangers is always a worthwhile exercise, for sometimes a whitefront, or perhaps a couple of bean geese, may be mixed among them. North European bean geese are uncommon visitors now, but whitefronted geese from Greenland

Some greylags are Scottish breeders, but most are drawn to nest in the distant northlands. *Scotland in Focus/Ken Taylor.*

gather on Islay, where not long ago they held centre stage in a fierce debate over the digging of distillery peat in their feeding grounds. Among the gaggles on the ground, the main distinguishing mark is the white blaze above their bills.

Even as the first willow warblers are arriving from the south, the goose skeins continue their northwards passage, mingling the sounds of departing winter with those of unfolding spring. Easter is a time when I enjoy a visit to Achiltibuie in Wester Ross. There the black and white forms of barnacle geese graze among the sprouting rushes of croftlands that stretch below the township to the shore, yelping like packs of dogs at any disturbance, real or imagined.

These are essentially western geese in Scotland. Their main haunts are the Solway marshes, like Caerlaverock, where the entire Spitzbergen breeding population has its traditional wintering grounds, and Loch Gruinart on Islay, the chief wintering centre of the Greenland flock. At both places, the spectacle of thousands of these smart 'black' geese on the ground or on the wing is one of Scotland's finest wildlife spectacles.

In days long gone, the sudden autumn arrival and spring departure of the barnacle geese were viewed with interest. At a time when bird migration was little understood, the curious legend of the seaside-haunting fowls was born. They couldn't hatch from eggs like other wildfowl, it was claimed, but must surely be spawned out of barnacles along the shore. After all, didn't they just suddenly appear along the coast each year? This was good news for the food-loving prelates of old, whose consciences needn't be troubled by eating flesh on a fast day. With such an origin the barnacle goose must surely be classed as fish rather than fowl!

Spring on the high hills

HILL walking may not be an option for every birdwatcher who visits the West in April, and there's no pleasure in falling into the countless sappy peat hags that flank the slopes. But on fine days I find a thrill in climbing high above the sea lochs of that fretted western rim, hoping always for a glimpse of peregrine or eagle. Sometimes I'm lucky and see one, occasionally both.

If the large birds of prey don't oblige, then sometimes the smallest

Purple saxifrage: bright jewel of lofty rock faces. *Douglas Willis.*

does, and a merlin glides swiftly across the dark face of the moor. Or perhaps the reward for the slog across leg-aching peat hags will be a moment of close contact with some deer, flashing white rumps signalling their flight across the brow of the hill.

In shaded mossy places beneath the summit crags, there's one April treasure that's worth all the foot-squelching upwards slog to see. In recessed crevices where the sweet song of the ring ouzel echoes among the rocks and dripping water glistens against green cushions of moss, cascades of bright purple saxifrage lighten the darkness and fairly take your breath away. One day near the month's end, while climbing a craggy face where the saxifrage blooms, I disturbed a pair of snow buntings among the jumble of frost-shattered rock. Perhaps they were prospecting for a nest site, for a few stay to breed each summer on our high tops. The cock bird had replaced the snowflake feathering of winter with the striking black and white of his breeding plumage. Saxifrage and snow bunting together: two rare mountain jewels in a setting of incomparable beauty.

46

Woodland creeper

THE birds that frequent our gardens sometimes pay a high price for their board, falling victim to marauding cats or flying into window panes. At home we're used to young sparrows and the occasional robin thinking that our windows are open spaces to be dashed through at the highest possible speed, then suffering the inevitable consequences. In a wooded park in Denmark, I saw a building with large paper cut-outs of flying birds of prey pasted to the inside of tall windows as a deterrent to small birds intent on flying into the glass, and by all accounts it was highly successful.

I'd never thought of tree creepers sharing the same fate till one day I was handed a fresh little corpse found under a window in the village and was surprised to find that the mousey creeper of the woodlands is really a mottled mixture of grey, brown and light russet feathering, while the pale underparts had almost a silvery sheen about them. The tree creeper's bill is slightly downturned at the end for gouging out any gollochs or whatever crawly protein may be lurking behind the bark. Occasionally we enjoy the brief company of one in our garden, but we have too few trees to keep them. But in the right kind of setting they may be persuaded to accept a narrow nest box fixed against the trunk of a tree, with a sideways slit of a hole that resembles a natural crevice.

To feed or not to feed?

IN the garden, the worst is past and the great bird-table feeding debate hinges on what's best done at this time of year: whether to carry on stocking up with food and filling the nut bags, or to scale the whole operation down. Opponents of the idea of late feeding suggest that parent birds may do harm to their youngsters by cramming peanuts down hungry throats. Others would argue that the birds know what's best for their growing broods. On balance, I'm inclined to think that it's better to let them get on with the job themselves as nature intended, collecting their food from a variety of sources. Nevertheless, I like to keep some contact with the individuals who have brightened the darker days of our winter garden, by putting out small pieces of soaked brown bread on the windowsill, an offer which chaffinches and sparrows find difficult to refuse.

Perversely, just when the summer warblers are filtering back from their African haunts, the ones which occasionally spend the winter in our northern gardens forsake us altogether, as the urge comes upon them to depart and find a mate. Blackcaps are warblers worth watching for these days, having recently become regular winterers throughout Scotland, a few Continental birds opting to stop off in the autumn and chance their luck in northern gardens.

Blackcaps are just what their name would suggest — little grey birds with jet black caps, though only the cocks actually answer to that description. Their consorts have a chestnut crown. In recent winters we've had both sexes around our garden, and surprisingly successful they become, flying off with most un-warbler-like beaksful of soaked bread. Last winter a chiffchaff also decided to spend the winter months with us, a tiny grey bird much like the more familiar willow warbler in appearance, but with dark, almost black, legs. Predictably, however, as April days began to lengthen, the lodger forsook our tended patch for the call of some wilder place.

This is the month for keeping an eye on nestboxes installed around the garden. Apart from the conservation value of a box or two, watching the comings and goings of house-hunting, and the convoluted relationships that attend it, may be more intriguing than any episode of *Dallas*, and guaranteed more true to life! By now the garden birds will have done a lot of nest-site prospecting, responding instinctively to the lengthening of the days and the increase in natural food supplies.

Run rabbit!

RABBITS have a reputation for being nervous creatures, fleeing at the first sight of approaching humanity. But they can be trusting animals, too, as friends of mine have discovered around their home.

Their red sandstone cottage lies at the opening of a small tree-filled valley, but to the front is a large grassy space where rabbits are seldom in short supply. At a glance, the scampering forms may all seem to look the same, but over the years my friends have come to recognise many individuals. Nothing unusual in that, perhaps, but what is unusual is the fact that the rabbits come when they're called, and even more remarkable is that they accept titbits of bread from the hand.

Whenever a stranger such as myself appears, they're reluctant to perform, but given time to settle they're not so bashful. Their lives aren't lived in any random kind of pattern, but according to strictly observed rules of place and position within their society, and woe betide any individual who does not toe the official rabbit line.

The arrival of a stranger in their midst creates no little upset, a fact I was able to witness one March evening from the large sitting-room window. The trees outside were bare of leaf and the light was beginning to fail. A buzzard wheeled low over the feeding area, sending the browsing rabbits in all directions in mad panic, but the danger soon passed and one by one the brown shapes appeared from their hidey holes.

In the midst of the mass exodus, one animal stood its ground: a large, long-eared black beast which must have escaped from a hutch in the village for it was extremely tame and seemed to have lost the instinctive urge to flee from danger. After a while, the mass nibbling continued, but every now and again one would break away and put the dark stranger to flight. Round and round they ran, the chaser catching up every now and again to give the fugitive a well-positioned nip. The result was that the fur had really been flying and the poor thing had tufts of hair missing all over, each one a painful reminder that a stranger in the rabbit ranks had better watch out!

A funny thing happened on the way to the lek . . .

IN places where forest gives way to open moor, the blackcock gather for their spectacular display. The chosen spot of these male black grouse is known as a lek, and there the red-wattled birds assemble at first light, puffed up with pride and prancing and parading in one of the most entrancing wildlife displays it's possible to see. As stylised in form as Sumo wrestlers in their circle, the puffed-up blackcock at their lek have impressed more than the nearby greyhens, for generations of Scottish birdwatchers have ensconced themselves in some suitable spot to view the performance. It's difficult to translate the strange sound of the lek, but W. Kenneth Richmond, who studied lekking blackcock in the Loch Ard area over many years, said it sounded to his ear like 'A stoup of sherry for Charrlie, a stoup of sherry for Charrlie, a stoup. . . .'

They say that lightning never strikes in the same place twice, but after my experiences at a blackcock lek I wouldn't be too sure. On the first occasion, the friend who was driving me to the lek fell foul of the law around 2 a.m. by driving at high speed through the streets of Aberdeen so as to reach the hide before daybreak. 'An far micht ye be gyaun in sic a rush at this time o' nicht?' enquired the burly bobby as he stepped out of his white Jaguar. Somehow the answer he got, including the detailed ongoings of blackcock at the lek, seemed only to confuse him, for he let us off with a cautionary 'Ah weel, awa ye go . . . An dinna dee't again!'

On another occasion, an early morning car run to a Deeside lek brought a flashing blue light swiftly up behind us and an enforced stop, the police on this occasion being hot on the trail of a stolen car of the same description as ours. They, too, seemed singularly bemused by the explanation of our nocturnal journeying!

Bonny birks

As the month wears through, a green haze begins to form among the larches as bursting buds respond to the season. Birches, too, take on new life as emerging leaves unfurl out of tightly-rolled buds. A North-east angler assured me that 'fan the leaves on the birks are the size o a moosie's lug' it's worth being out on the river. Personally, I've sometimes viewed that first budding with rather different motives, tapping the lower trunks for that ultra-clear rising sap to transform it into the highly drinkable birch sap wine. Now I'm relieved of the bother of this April ritual, for such is the appeal of this delectable wine that the Moniack Castle winery near Beauly produces it commercially.

Few spring sights are more stirring than that of fresh-leaved birches. The Birks of Aberfeldy. *Scotland in Focus/Roger Fox.*

Not far from Moniack, up the Beauly River, the waterside trees found fame in a fiddle tune by the master composer Scott Skinner who, when a road roller plunging down a bank destroying some silver birches, was moved to pen that lovely air 'The Weeping Birches of Kilmorack'. The same pale-barked trees also lend a spring delight to the Birks of Aberfeldy, downstream from Loch Tay where a fine nature walk provides a pleasant woodland experience among the birches and other mixed trees both at this time of early freshness and through the summer days.

Hunchbacked heron

ON lengthening April nights I like to take a late walk along the shore, listening to the lapping of waves against shingle, and the piping of oystercatchers as they bicker over their allocation of tideline. Often I glimpse a lone heron standing motionless in the moonlight, and no doubt observing my approach long before I notice him. Sometimes he stays his ground, hunchbacked and miserable-looking, but more often he makes himself scarce, flying with slow down-flapping wings and a complaining scraach. On the east coast he's the craggit heron, but on the Gaelic west he's Chorra-Ghritheac, a fine-sounding name for a fine-looking bird.

In the Fairy Glen

IN the Fairy Glen near my home (there are several others scattered about the country), fine April days fill the tree-lined defile with a new greenness that fairly lifts the heart. The birches, larch and a few scattered old pines crowd around a landscape that is strangely raw by contrast. Above the gully of the Muckle Red Den, reddish clay pillars form, then fade and form again as boulders in the clay shield the soft clay underneath from heavy rain. Earth pillars (for so they're called,

Grey heron: patient fisherman of burn and lochside. *Scotland in Focus/Ken Taylor.*

Curious earth pillars rise starkly skywards from the Black Isle's
Fairy Glen. *Douglas Willis.*

despite their clay composition) are unusual features in this country,
though I've often been fascinated by them on moraine-covered slopes
in the high Alps. With a boulder perched on top, it's hardly surprising
that the French know these landscape curiosities as 'ladies with hats'.

Early one dewy April morning I came upon a fox curled up
beneath the precipitous edge of the clay arête. At first he seemed
oblivious of my presence, but then his ears pricked and his head
turned. The two sharp eyes glowed like heated coals in the morning
light, and he was off like a shot, leaving only a musky memory behind
in the heavy air of morning.

A few of the glen's larches are old and spreading, their trunks
bent by the urge to keep growing upright as their roots slip steadily
downhill. The larch is one of our finest spring trees, giving the lie to
the notion that all conifers are evergreen, for now it sports all its fresh

54

finery in a great burst of tufted needles. Introduced into this country from mountain Europe as an ornamental tree, larch was later widely planted for commercial purposes, particularly on the Perthshire estates of the Dukes of Atholl. It was there that a cross between the European and Japanese larch was first noted near Dunkeld, providing foresters with a hardier hybrid for their planting schemes.

For years, at the Banffshire fishing village of Macduff, you could stop and marvel at the outdoor craftsmanship of the boat builders with their ancient adzes, skilfully shaping well-seasoned larch timbers into the curving elegance of a fishing-boat hull. Now they're screened from the road within a covered yard where their time-honoured craft continues unseen, hopefully not threatened by future cuts in the fishing fleet.

'For lo the winter is past . . .'

FROM the earliest days of animal husbandry, the sight of newborn spring lambs has cheered the soul, a lively symbol of the passing of winter and the assurance of a new life cycle begun. Now, with the popularity of the stocky Suffolk breed among lowland flockmasters, early lambings are commonplace, but still good for a newspaper photograph or two. In recent times, some variety has come into the

A new generation of Cheviots, free from the rigours of
'lambing storms'. *Scotland in Focus/John Forsyth.*

spring lambing picture with the sight of delightfully mottled Jacob's lambs thrusting themselves enthusiastically under their dams in search of a drink. These four-horned animals are in direct line of descent from the old spotted sheep of Biblical times. Here and there another rare breed or two puts in an appearance, but somehow I can never reconcile the sight of a North Ronaldsay ewe and lamb on lush lowland pastures as far removed as it's possible to be from the seaweed-strewn rocks of their native Orkney shore. Far-flung North Ronaldsay I remember for all sorts of reasons, but the multicoloured beasts on its seashore beneath the high sheep dyke are not easily forgotten, not least when they spring from rock to tide-washed rock with glaikit looks and great trails of salty tangle dripping from their mouths.

Setting up home

BY now the neighbourhood blackbirds and song thrushes are well into nest building. Some places in our garden appeal to both, the favourite being a bushy golden cypress with a succession of thrush and blackie nests over the years. Suddenly, the value of having a shallow corner in the garden pool is demonstrated by the blackies who spend hours removing muddy green slime to plaster into the inside of their nests. Dunnocks like to seek out more secluded nesting places, so if space permits, it's useful to have a fairly dense conifer or two about the garden, precisely for offering nesting accommodation to such househunters.

By the third week we start looking for our returning swallows. Of all nature's predictable patterns, the return of the swallows is perhaps the most uplifting. With no suitable nesting premises to offer, our garden is quickly bypassed, but the village joiner's workshop draws them like a magnet, several pairs setting up home in the rafters above the lathes and piles of shavings.

House martins arrive a little later, quickly beginning their renovations or starting new mud cup constructions under desirable eaves. It's interesting to keep a note of these first arrival dates so that they can be compared with years past and years to come, and many folk take delight in telling me of the swallow's arrival dates of years gone by.

The swallow's arrival is a much looked-for symbol of advancing spring.
Scotland in Focus/Eric Middleton.

Though April may be well advanced before the swallow's coming, it's this one eagerly awaited return that somehow sets the seal on the season, a sign that although we may view the countryside year within the bounds of our human calendar, it's nature's own seasonal round that gives our country places their ongoing patterns.

The Caledonian pine

FROM time to time I meet with a red squirrel scampering up the flaky red bark of a venerable pine in the mixed tree growth of the Fairy Glen, but they prefer the dense stands of planted pines in the nearby plantations.

A few of our older local forests have come, in their maturity, to resemble the old Highland pinewoods with their rich understorey of heather, juniper and blaeberry. Great-spotted woodpeckers find these places much to their liking, prising off the great bark flakes with

hammering bills. In breeding plumage they're a splendid sight in chequered black and white markings and bright red rump, flighting from tree to tree with a sharp *kik* call, then sending their drumming calls echoing among the tree tops.

Strongly linked to the old Caledonian pine forest, the great spotted woodpecker nearly disappeared as the once vast northern wildwood fell to axe and fire. Happily, it has benefited from the spread of commercial conifer plantings, and is widely seen once more. After years of neglect, the ancient Caledonian pines have found their champions in foresters like Finlay Macrae in Inverness-shire's Glen Affric, determined that this living heritage should have a true value set upon it. And recognising the unique wildlife and landscape interest of the surviving remnant forest, the RSPB in recent years acquired as a nature reserve a large tract of the Abernethy Forest in the shadow of the snowcapped Cairngorms. Where the old pines thrive in last refuges like Glen Affric, Rothiemurchus on Speyside and Ballochbuie on Deeside, I value a few moments standing among them in the freshness of a new season for that sense of continuity with a countryside past which they so powerfully evoke.

Old pines, Wester Ross. Long-lived survivors of countless passing seasons. *Douglas Willis.*

M A Y

'Ye think the Gabs o' Mey are past?
Weel, jist ee wyte ma loon,
An' in anither week or twa,
Ye'll get the Gabs o' June.'

PETER BUCHAN

FOR country folk the piercing cold of the 'Gab o' May' was a sharp reminder of the vagaries of our Scottish climate. That there was such a vernacular description for this unwelcome (literally 'open-mouthed') spell of early May weather confirms just how often spring's progress may be slowed at this time. For the weather-watching pessimist, like the one in Peter Buchan's poem, such an aftertaste of winter might indeed seem like a bad omen for the weather pattern to come.

On the whole, however, May is a month to savour spring freshness; a time for woodland walks and appreciation of a new season's growth; time to enjoy the close company of the birds. To walk among the trees on a fresh May morning is to sense the strength of nature's renewal, to see the promise of spring fulfilled in its infinite variety of form. To be surrounded by the leafy growth and fresh flowering of the woodland floor, and to sense the frenetic activity of the birds, is to come closer to the sheer power of nature than at any other time in the course of the year.

Rites of spring

THE first of the month is traditionally the most auspicious time for washing your face in the morning dew. Outside the Black Isle village of Avoch, the first Sunday in May is the duly observed date for a walk to Craiguck, a clootie well where generations of local folk have tied up their rag offerings on the branches of the tree above the spring. Last

Munlochy Bay, Ross-shire, its flanks brightened by the yellow impact of oil seed rape. *Douglas Willis.*

year an unrelenting downpour of rain was making crumpled confetti of the gean blossoms on the road to Craiguck, but I was glad to see that it had failed to dampen the enthusiasm of two of my young pupils from the village. In time-honoured fashion they had walked along the shore to tie up their own cloots and ones given to them by their mothers to hang above this ancient water issue.

I find myself observing my own rites of spring at this most appealing time of the countryside year, and one of these is my annual quest for the orange-tip butterfly. Orange-tips are beautiful little white butterflies whose name is descriptive of their appearance. They used to be scarce in the north, but in defiance of the trend towards butterfly decline, they seem to be increasing their range. On sunny days in early May they seek out the fresh flowering of the mauve-bloomed lady's smock, performing their twinkling love flight over the damp spots where it grows. In our own garden we much enjoy the lovely double form of the flower once so beloved of old cottage gardeners, but although orange-tips often flutter past on fine May days they're real sun-worshippers and steadfastly avoid the shady spot where our lady's smock flourishes, preferring to perform their orange-tipped twinkling in the open sunshine.

Highland folk once called the defiant cock capercaillie the 'horse of the woods'. *Scotland in Focus/Laurie Campbell.*

Horse of the woods

WE'RE fortunate in our Scottish heritage of woodland birds, from the tiny, bright-crowned goldcrest to the giant capercaillie. The capercailzie (old Scots spelling) has its home in the coniferous forests, whether the ancient Caledonian pines of Strathspey or the mature commercial plantations that chequer our uplands. It's easy to see why the bird's old Highland name was 'horse of the woods', for a full-grown cock bird is an impressive sight. And what's more, they've a reputation for showing strangers the door of their territories, one celebrated bird in a Perthshire glen being a bittie more ambitious than most, by attempting to see a Landrover off his patch!

One dewy May morning, I had an interesting face-to-face encounter with a territorial caper along a Black Isle forest ride. A felling squad had removed some edging larch some time before, and it was alongside one of their piles of neatly stacked logs that I first noticed the dark turkey-sized object waddling in my direction. Through binoculars, the morning sheen on the caper's upper body became a green iridescence, offsetting the red wattles around a sharp, glaring eye.

For a moment, he stopped his morning dander, determined, it seemed, to stand his ground, or perhaps not sure just what to do next. Then, to my surprise, he proceeded to waddle closer still, craning his neck from one side to the other. By now I was beginning to ponder the politics of a strategic withdrawal, but I needn't have worried, for his nerve broke and he was up and away, clattering through the pines and thus sparing me any indignity.

It was a sad day when clearance of the ancient Caledonian pines put paid to the native caper stock. Today's birds are mostly derived from Scandinavian imports released at Taymouth in Perthshire last century. But now, after a hugely successful recolonisation, the capercaillie's fortunes seem to have taken a downturn in many areas, so it's good news that the Forestry Commission is managing a forest area at Strath Rory in the Eastern Highlands with the needs of this magnificent bird specifically in mind. Capercaillies are certainly worth looking for, but seeing them is very much a case of being in the right quiet place at the right time. If someone has passed that way just before, they're unlikely still to be about, so an early walk among the trees is often the best bet.

Heritage among the trees

OUR surviving mixed woodlands are a rich natural heritage, deserving better than the treatment they received in the past. In the rich environments of wooded nature reserves like Killiecrankie, and of Inversnaid on the shores of Loch Lomond, the drumming of woodpeckers is fitting backcloth for such summer migrant gems as pied flycatcher and redstart.

By contrast, conifer plantings stand poor comparison in form and colour and boast less variety of birds. But there's more to forests than

Golden eagle: a striking symbol of the wild Highlands.
Scotland in Focus/Laurie Campbell.

just a lot of trees and birds, for many plantations have been established in places where folk once lived.

Rosal, an abandoned crofting township in north Sutherland, is a history-steeped spot hemmed in by forest plantings. While the nineteenth-century clearance of Strathnaver continues to fire national passion, Rosal is now just an island of lighter green among the surrounding dark conifers. On the site of the old township, nature seems intent on taking the place back to herself, for the ruined homes of the evicted families sport a growth of lichens and moss, helping to mellow a place that was poignantly quiet when last I visited it on an overcast day in May.

In the profound peace it was almost a relief to hear the enthusiastic cadences of an early willow warbler mingling with the echoed rushing of a burn. In a strange sort of way, the peacefulness seems almost to speak out the life and times of the hardy folk who harvested their corn and herded their black cattle there, till the thatch was burned from their homes to clear them from a land that was theirs by right but not by law. Now the crumbling croft ruins and vague imprints of the old cultivation rigs kindle the imagination, recalling everyday life as it may have been in that Highland strath before the Cheviot sheep displaced the folk.

Silent as the ruins below, an eagle soared overhead, pinions flexed in the updraught. Like the folk of the glens, the golden eagle also had cause to regret the high-handed style of estate management, falling foul of a gamekeeping crusade intent on ridding the land of 'vermin', especially anything with a hooked beak. In reality, the eagle is often a carrion feeder, attracted to sheep and deer carcases. The Strathnaver eagle's sights would certainly have been set on something larger than the agitated sandpipers which bobbed along the burnside. Well does 'Kittie neddie', the sandpiper's old Scots name, match its repetitive calling along the summer straths.

Back at the mouth of the Naver, a greenshank added its nervous *teu, teu, teu* call over grassy slopes yellow-peppered with May primroses and pollen-dusted dwarf pussy willows. A nearby roadside quarry yielded an unexpected bonus: a single blackcock, resplendent in glossy black breeding plumage with a lyre tail that would have done justice to a regimental bonnet.

This was a northern day to remember. But above the recollection of soaring eagle, flighting greenshank and lyre-tailed blackcock, one enduring image long remained: an image of the deserted homeland of a forgotten Highland folk, and of the lonely silence broken by the haunting call of a nesting curlew. Early summer at Rosal can be a season of special attraction, the sad history of the place now recalled in interpretative panels on the site.

Rooftop rowdies

SILENCE is a virtue unrecognised by our village gulls. There was a time when seagulls really were birds of sea and shore. Then along came a wasteful urban society, and the gulls moved in to feast on the leavings. Inverness's seashore rubbish tip has enjoyed the dubious distinction of hosting the biggest seagull party in the land. The result is that, not far away as the gull flies, our Black Isle villages have to thole more than their share of nesting nuisances on the rooftops. The rowdies' unwelcome contributions to the dawn chorus shatter the May mornings, and I've never learned to appreciate being woken up by barnacle-encrusted shells clattering down the roof-tiles as a frustrated gull abandons its attempt to evict the hermit crab occupants.

When I lived in a North-east coastal town, I used to trap gulls for ringing, each bird being given a numbered metal leg ring with the address of the British Museum so that its future movements might hopefully be recorded. In those days, weekend fishing-boat sailings were unheard of, the fleet remaining resolutely in port till the very last second of the Sabbath day was past. By Monday, the harbour-haunting gulls were beside themselves with hunger. For the price of a few herring, dozens of gulls could be caught in a baited wire trap in the garden.

The method was simple in the extreme: throw a few fish inside, wait for the squawking blizzard to descend, then haul the door shut with a string. In their panic to get airborne, the gulls would regurgitate their newly-swallowed meals, a fact that greatly suited my impecunious student state, for the same fish could be used over and over again till several journeys up and down the gulls' gullets took effect, and the unsavoury bait had finally to be disposed of.

Ringing returns reflected their unadventurous lives spent scrounging around the local fishing harbours. But they made up for it in the manner of their dying, which sometimes involved mass suicides by suffocation, performed by diving into deep fish barrels, Kamikaze fashion, or getting themselves flattened under lorry wheels at the harbour when the weight of fish inside them prevented a quick take-off.

The herring gull is the species most often involved in rooftop squats, but its neat little kittiwake cousin has also found seaside buildings a substitute for cliffs, some enterprising birds at North Berwick discovering that high windows with a sea view are an ideal place for bringing up a seafaring family. I'm a great admirer of kittiwakes, but if we're to have roof-nesting birds at all, then I'd much prefer the storks which I've enjoyed watching on red-tiled rooftops abroad. But since the last Scottish nesting of storks was on top of St Giles in Edinburgh in 1416, it looks as if we'll just have to make do with our antisocial seagull squatters!

Some of the young rooftop gulls invariably come to grief, and I dread the inevitable phone calls at this time, asking if I would be interested in taking charge of a waif that has made a premature descent. I politely point out the questionable long-term joys of bringing up a seagull orphan, citing the case of the North-east lady who took in a gull lodger and still had the dubious pleasure of its company nearly four decades and countless cans of catfood later!

Leave well alone!

As a general rule, young birds of any sort should be left well alone at this time. Even if they appear to be abandoned, the chances are that they're part of a brood that has scattered through the area, and the parents will be aware of their location. Baby owls, crows and jackdaws are often mistakenly 'rescued' in this way. In fact, feeding and repatriating them to the wild is a highly skilled task.

Miracle of spring

MY friend Jimmy Steven has a passion for Clydesdale horses. On his Black Isle croft he keeps a couple of mares, sending them away at auspicious times in a cattle float to some approved stallion suitor furth of the peninsula. On a sunny and mild May evening last year I had a telephone call to announce that the large lady in waiting, the older mare, had been safely delivered of a son — a finely marked colt — and would we like to come across to see it?

My wife and I needed no persuading, for it's not every day that you have the treat of seeing one of nature's real spring miracles. When we arrived the mare was cropping the grass in a small field close to the house, her son stretched out beside her in the warmth of the evening sun. Every now and again mother would gently nudge his soft chestnut and white flanks with her great hairy lips as son dreamed dreams of his next feed to the background lullaby of evening skylark song. In a while the colt responded by struggling to achieve a state of balance on top of decidedly shaky legs. But, to me, the most remarkable thing of all was that when he did rise the height of his knees above the ground exactly matched that of his mother's, for the height of the animal is determined long before the development of the rest of its body.

Ben, the family's black and white collie dog, was taking a real proprietorial interest in the new arrival, rushing over to the foal as soon as he realised we were headed in that direction, and lying close to the towering mother who paid singularly little attention to his presence. When a foal is in the womb, I was told, there's a small soft pad inside its mouth. In days when the working horse dominated the farm scene, and the Horseman's Word mystically bound those who swore into it, tradition had it that if this birth offering was removed and dried it could be shaped into a whistle that would achieve almost magical rapport with the beast from which it came.

Out of interest, Jimmy had kept the thing after the birth and dried it off, and was about to show it to me when we discovered that a hungry crow had decided that the talisman might be worth assessing for its edibility, and had departed with it in its beak!

The morning after, I happened to be in Speyside and chanced upon Ian MacInnes at Carrbridge with his great Clydesdale horse, Bob. His working life had begun alongside a timber contractor's horse and now the wheel has come full circle, for when I saw him he was looking after the massive gelding at the Forest Heritage Centre. As we talked, the nearby steam traction engine hissed and tooted, but the gentle beast didn't so much as flicker one of his great eyelids. In a moment he was harnessed into his working rig, powerfully dragging the felled timber in the pinewood's resinous air.

Rose linties and white blackies

FOR everything there is a season, said the Old Testament preacher, but in nature it can be said that for everything there's a reason, too. So, it's no strange thing to encounter quite large flocks of linnets well into May, long after other small birds have paired up and settled down to nest. These little finches are adapted to feeding their young on specific seed crops, so the exact timing of their nesting season is determined by the availability of the right brand of baby food.

Few sights are cheerier than that of a pink-breasted rose lintie pouring out his song from the top of a flowering whin bush. One early summer, two white fledglings appeared in our local golf course's crop of linnet youngsters. On closer inspection, however, their plumage pattern showed vaguely through, like a pale grey shadow against almost silvery body feathering. Understandably, white blackbirds tend to hit the local headlines, for they're such a contradiction in name as well as colour. Abnormal plumage isn't really that uncommon, though. In the course of the last few years, I've seen an oatmeal-coloured curlew, a white collared dove, a near-white ringed plover, a white-headed house sparrow, and an assortment of piebald blackies.

An oddly-feathered bird in the garden can be very useful, making it possible to check on the individual's habits, and this will almost certainly cause a rethink of the numbers of birds about the place. 'The' blue tits, for example, may turn out to be a whole lot of different birds doing the rounds of the neighbourhood. A deformity can be a useful distinguishing characteristic, too. In this way we know that one of our rooftop gulls with a missing foot has been around for at least sixteen years.

Pinkie braes

ALONG the eastern fringe, primroses are sometimes called spinks. In other places 'pinkie braes' were spots where, somewhat perversely, drifts of yellow primroses carpeted the slopes. On fine May days I feel drawn to walk among the primrose patches of some grassy cliff or by a lively burn with the flowers clinging to its banks. The Preaching

In all of spring's flowering, nothing quite matches a bright primrose patch. *Scotland in Focus/Laurie Campbell.*

Burn at Ferintosh in the Black Isle is such a place in which I like to wander, conjuring up pictures of those long gone days when the May flowers were silent witnesses to the great open-air preachings and sacraments that made this lowly burn famous throughout the north.

Bountiful burns

IT'S a pity that so many of our lowland burns have been so badly polluted that they've lost their once rich interest. In schooldays we had a ritual of heading burnwards on fine May days, armed with 'bandy' nets and jam jars with string tied round the rim in search of whatever fish life we might find. They were bountiful places, where sometimes we might chance on a real prize — a water hen's nest on an overhanging branch, filled so full of brown-spotted eggs that you wondered if one bird could possibly have laid them all. As often as not the small fish would easily elude our nets, while their larger relations mocked us with their plopping in the deep water flow.

70

Watching a fine spotted trout among the weed in a summer burn is a therapeutic sight. Head pointed upstream, it seems to hang, suspended in the flow. At a cottage where an old lady had lived there was a deep outside well reputed to contain a giant trout, but we could never see it against the bright reflection of sky and our own peering boyish faces. There may well have been one, for such lodgers in the water supply were once common enough, the fish consuming the varied creepie crawlies that tumbled down the well.

Some Highland lochs support stocks of charr, a reminder of days when the climate had an Arctic touch to it. Charr are beautiful creatures, with striking red flanks and belly, though their finery soon fades when they are taken from their cold watery element. It's often in the charr lochs that there lurk the giant 'ferox' trout; grotesquely overgrown monsters that feast on their smaller relations and grace many a glass case in fishing lodges and hotels throughout the Highlands.

Doos and doocots

NOT far from my home there's a sea cave that must have been occupied by rock doves for generations. The evidence is an impressive stalagmite of pigeon droppings beneath a favourite roosting ledge. In recent years ornithologists have been bemoaning the loss of purity in the rock dove stocks as waifs and strays from homing pigeon races throw in their lot with their not-so-civilised relations, soon adding their own contribution to the motley colourings of the flock.

To judge by the success of toon doos, a city centre represents a reasonably close approximation to a sea cliff with all its rock ledges and roosting places. Wherever food supplies appear, the pigeons are quick to descend from whatever irreverent perch they've been adorning. Toon doos are great levellers, perching on monarch and vagrant alike in parks and streets where statues provide a convenient perching place and down-and-outs share their crumbs with the birds.

Lairds with an eye to the culinary qualities of a fine pigeon squab weren't slow to erect their doocots throughout the lowland farmlands, never mind that the birds might find their pickings on some cottar's meagre patch. Doocots add great interest to the Scottish country scene. Sometimes they were incorporated into fine farm steadings, frequently over an arch, like the one above the elegant curve of farm offices in Aden Country Park in Aberdeenshire. But often they're fine-looking stone-built affairs that add a welcome touch of the past to today's intensively-worked farmlands. Whether built to one of the classic lectern-shaped plans or to a beehive design, doocots share the same general characteristics. The inside walls are lined with nests that look like stone boxes. They were reached by a revolving interior ladder called a potence (French for a gallows), another word to add to ashet, chaumer and the like, acquired in the days of the Auld Alliance. Though the flesh of fledgling pigeon squabs was the main output of the doocots, there was another much prized by-product. Doo dung had valued fertilising powers and was reputed to be especially efficacious with onions, the irony being that the pigeons were helping to grow the vegetables that would be an accompaniment to their own consumption!

Some doocots are great visitor attractions, such as the prominent round white tower on the hill at Boath in Morayshire from which Montrose oversaw the battle of Auldearn. Like the one at Boath, the imposing Phantassie doocot at East Linton in East Lothian is also in the care of the National Trust for Scotland. Its most striking feature is its hooded top above a beehive base. Phantassie Doocot forms a fitting complement to the nearby water-worked Preston Mill, also a National Trust for Scotland property.

Splashing out

BIRDS enjoy a really good bath, though avian bathing can cover a multitude of things. Sparrows like nothing better than having a dust version — especially in the middle of a row of newly sown seeds, while jackdaws have an addiction to smoke bathing, sitting on a chimney pot and letting the reek rise through their plumage. But for most birds there's nothing quite like a good splash and a dook, so that a garden pool becomes a real neighbourhood mecca.

At its simplest, a pool may be an upturned dustbin lid sunk into the ground, but at its best it will be a proper pond, with all the interest which that can bring. Modern tough plastic liners can be used to create a pool within hours. In a small, newly created pool in our front garden we were surprised to see water boatmen rising to the surface within days, and within weeks a whole lot of pond skaters — 'washer wifies' I first learned to call them — deftly skating over the surface.

Goldfish and rich pond life don't really go together, for the fish will consume the natural interest. They also attract predators. Blackbirds may seem unlikely consumers of small goldfish, but they are. In an Edinburgh garden, a suburban fox was suspected of removing some precious ornamental fish from the shallows of a large pond. Herons are sometimes tempted in to a larger pool, and after a daring evening raid on our back garden pool, our giant, sixteen-year-old goldfish was abducted to make an ignominious last journey headfirst down the gullet of a hungry gull. Birds will flock to a pool in dry weather, but steep sides are disastrous when the water level falls, so the edge should be shelving, or a stone conveniently placed to avoid bathing tragedies.

Buzzing bum bees

IN my childhood days we never spoke of bumble bees. The big black and yellow hairy things that droaned over our heads on summer days were always bum bees. We lived in a certain awe of the creatures, imagining that they might inflict some terrible stinging torture if you were to poke at their nests. As a result, we tended to give them a wide berth, though there was a daredevil satisfaction in catching one in a jam jar for a minute or two and holding it to your ear while the angry buzzing inside fairly made the glass dirl. For some unexplained reason, the bees featured in our playground play, as bairns teased one another with the refrain 'Ye canna catch me for a big bum bee!'

Male chauvinism has no part in the bumble bee's world, for the males are subservient creatures in a world dominated by the queen, and all are doomed to die as the days shorten and temperatures fall, leaving only the queen bee to hibernate and thus ensure the continuity of the race. Their nests are fairly small affairs, serviced by the workers which buzz clumsily around the entrance hole, usually in a grass bank. The buzz of activity that might attend some event like a country roup was well summed up in the analogy 'Like a githerin o bum bees roon a girsy dyke'.

High-rise flier

THE swift comes late to our Scottish towns, returning as May begins to advance, but, like the linnet, its ways are in tune with the providence of the season, for rising air temperatures bring the abundance of high-flying insects required to feed its young. Swifts are real masters of the air, screaming round high eaves and clock towers in the long summer evenings on scimitar wings styled for speed. I've only twice encountered a grounded swift, and on each occasion it was a surprise to see the almost legless feet, well adapted for clinging to stonework, but useless on the ground. It seems such a contradiction that an earthbound swift should be held so complete a prisoner by those same long wings that give it mastery of the skies above. In fact, all that's usually required to launch a healthy grounded swift is to toss it into the air, then watch it speed away heavenwards.

It's hardly surprising that the higher buildings of our old burgh centres are favourite nesting places of the swift, for they provide a good substitute for natural rock crevices. Swifts will come to nest boxes, but the entrance hole must be underneath, for they approach their nesting crevices directly from below. Swallows can also be encouraged to breed inside buildings where rafters are scarce, by tacking on small flat pieces of wood to form nesting platforms. While the appearance of a martin's mud cup in the eaves may be viewed with mixed feelings, the interest in seeing a brood being reared will amply repay the fall of droppings below. In any case, knocking down their nests and eggs is against the law. Simulated mud cups have been used with great success by house martins for many years and can now be obtained commercially.

Fence sitter

WHILE martin, swift and swallow have always nested well above the ground, the oystercatcher seems an unlikely candidate for joining their lofty lifestyle. Yet, during two Mays we watched a pair bring off young on the flat roof of our village school, till the cannibal herring gulls fed the baby oystercatchers to their own ravenous broods. On

Opting for the high life, an oystercatcher's nest in the rotted
top of a fence post. *Douglas Willis*.

hospital and college roofs in Aberdeen, oystercatchers have long
accepted the pebble-strewn surfaces as an elevated beach, sending
their shrill piping down to echo through wards and lecture rooms.

Even in the countryside, oystercatchers have been taking to the
high life, laying their eggs in the rotting hollow tops of fence strainer
posts. It seems a strange nesting place for a bird adapted to laying
among the pebbles of the seashore, but Scottish oystercatchers are an
enterprising lot, colonising country places long before their southern
counterparts. Fence-post nesting seems to be just the latest stage in
their gradual integration with the farming landscape. In terms of
freedom from predators, it's probably the case that a bird on the post
is worth two on the ground!

JUNE

'The yalla blossom's on the funn, o livrock-sang there's rowth...'

FLORA GARRY

*L*IKE the month that precedes it, June has a freshness that is destined to fade in the days of high summer. Month of longest evenings and high point in the countryside year, it seems now as if nature's pent-up energy must be dissipated before the summer solstice, and day length begins to wane once more. It's in the early days of the month that the last remnants of 'roch grun' which the improvers' ploughs failed to tame seem to burst into sheets of yellow flame in the mass flowering of the whins, recalling a Scottish countryside that has largely gone.

A golden curve of whins traces an embankment by the side of Loch Carron. *Douglas Willis.*

Seabird cities

PERHAPS nowhere is the month's exuberance more marked than at the great bird colonies of our coastal edge. These are splendid birdwatching sites to visit at this time of year. Along our Scottish coastline we're spoiled for choice, for there are so many classic seabird cities: the Shetland island of Noss with its white rows of gannets; Orkney's Marwick Head where fulmars cackle in the updraught of the sheer cliff face; Handa island on the west, with its great sandstone stack; Troup Head in Banffshire, overlooking tiny fisher villages that cling to the rock like the nesting birds themselves; the red granite Bullers of Buchan where the famous Dr Johnson made a characteristically verbose comment on its curious form; the pudding-stone cliffs of Fowlsheugh on the Kincardine coast; right down to the crowded guillemot ledges of St Abb's Head in the Borders.

They're all places of rare quality at this time when bird nesting activities are at their height, and to visit one can be a real highlight of the birdwatching year. At each, the calls of a myriad flighting birds echo above the sound of the swell below, and the fishy smell of the whitewash lifts on the updraught. It's hard to separate ornithology and geology here, for the seabirds line the ledges which centuries of battering by wind and salt spray have furrowed into the face of the rock.

It's worth sitting for a while on a clifftop to watch the way the birds conduct their affairs. Shags, with jaunty crests and beetle-green sheen, have a preference for the basement flats, often just out of reach of the surging swell. Kittiwakes — their name derived from their cliff-face calling — seek the noise and bustle of their own kind in their overcrowded tenements. Guillemots opt for a life of serried ranks along the narrowest of ledges, while fulmars enjoy the outlook from bijou residences along the upper cliff, commanding the best views across a lively community that is never quiet. It's also worth scanning the lines of guillemots for individuals with the curious comma-shaped eye marking or 'bridling', a characteristic that becomes ever more common the further north the colony lies.

Along the crowded cliffs, nature works some of her finest wildlife wonders. Kittiwakes cling to the merest suspicion of ledge. Guillemots have learned that laying eggs decidedly pointed at one end is an

Fulmar on the Shetland island of Unst, impassively viewing
the busy seabird scene. *Douglas Willis.*

insurance against loss, for a knocked egg merely spins round on the
bare rock, so avoiding a drop into oblivion.

At Fowlsheugh, perhaps my favourite seabird city of all, the bond
between birds and rock is even more intriguing. Millions of years ago,
the sediments which were to form the rock were full of rounded
boulders carried down by fast-flowing burns. Today's legacy is the
conglomerate, or pudding stone, where individual nesting sites have
been created by the fall-out of stones from the cliff face, leaving
empty sockets that make ideal nesting places. At the height of the
breeding season, the Fowlsheugh clifftop is a place to sit in restful
contemplation, listening to the echoing cacophony below, and hearing
occasionally the stony 'fruit' fall out of the pudding, released from its
ancient grip by the squabbling of the birds.

The Great Stack of Handa — a storeyed seabird city. *Douglas Willis.*

Flower of Scotland

JUNE'S clifftop experience is enriched by more than the birds, and it would be hard not to notice the wealth of wild flowers. It's not surprising that coastal plants should bloom so prolifically when so much seabird fertiliser is showered on them from above. Drifts of bright pink campion brighten the bottoms of northern geos, the yellow-flowered roseroot unfolds its succulent leaves out of narrow rock crevices. And thrift, the glory of the seaside with its sea pink rosettes, carpets clifftops and grassy ledges where comic-faced puffins gather, like a boorach of old men enjoying a good blether.

Of all the seaside plants, however, none can compare with *Primula scotica*, the national flower. The rare Scots primrose blooms in only one small part of the whole world, and it's our good fortune to have it along our northern coasts. A tiny gem of a plant, each perfect group of miniature purple flowers with bright yellow eye is held above a stem only an inch and a half or so in height. From Orkney's North Isles, by way of the high clifftops of Yesnaby on West Mainland, then across the stormy divide of the Pentland Firth to the Caithness and North Sutherland coast, the tiny Scots primrose blooms still in haunts which have been spared 'improvement'.

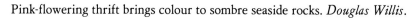

Pink-flowering thrift brings colour to sombre seaside rocks. *Douglas Willis.*

Real flower of Scotland, the tiny Primula scotica blooms only along northern coasts. *Scotland in Focus/Ken Taylor.*

On a brief trip to attend the induction of a minister friend to his new north-coast parish, I arrived early so that I might have a walk down the coast path to a spray-drenched bank where the primula grows. A couple of great skuas swooped half-heartedly as I walked the clifftop to the spot where the tiny flowers had opened above mealy leaf rosettes, each dusted in a frosty white bloom.

Having spent too long among the primulas, I found myself pushed for time to change into my best suit and head towards the little grey kirk where the service was soon to take place. Deciding on an alfresco wardrobe change, I selected a convenient peat stack and proceeded to step out of my trousers. Too late did I notice the intrigued looks at the window of the nearby cottage, the dumfoonert expression on the crofter wife's face revealing total amazement at such questionable ongoings on the way to the kirk.

With concern being expressed over the future of this national treasure, it's good news that the Scottish Wildlife Trust has recently acquired an Orkney reserve on the south island of Hoy, with the splendid name of the Hill of the White Hamars, and there the *Primula scotica* flowers along its high coast edge.

Escape from Sandaig

EVERYBODY knows that June can fall far short of its flaming reputation, but the east coast often puts a particular damper on the proceedings when a cold, clinging haar rolls in from the North Sea, blanketing the coastal fringe for hours, while places only a mile or two inland bask in the sunshine. It happens when air that is humid in its lower layers leaves the comparatively warm Continent and flows over the cooler North Sea. The air becomes saturated as it reaches the east coast and forms fog.

At times like this it's a treat to forsake the shrouded east and seek the sunshine of the west. On a foggy June morning, my wife and I did just that, heading past Loch Ness lay-bys already filling with hopeful Nessie-spotters, then through Glenmoriston to mountainous Kintail with its matching Five Sisters. It was just the right moment to appreciate the drifts of yellow-speared flag irises crowding every damp hillside hollow among fresh green bracken.

At the high-level car park above Bealach Ratagain, with its bird's-eye view down to Morvich and the otter-haunted head of Loch Duich, a whinchat sang his discordant song in defiance of a steady stream of visitors pausing to admire the view and allow overheated car engines to cool down after the fearsome ascent. Then, a little further on, we walked the winding forest track down to the Skye-facing shore where Gavin Maxwell once delighted to watch otters play.

Over on the little Sandaig Islands across the sound from Skye, some cows were placidly standing on the connecting strand. Their shaggy forebears swam the nearby Kylerhea narrows from the Misty Isle on their way to join the great southward cattle droves. But these less hirsute beasts clearly had no such ambitions, being content to wade up to their bovine oxters in the warm blue sea, or to browse among grey-lichened rocks and tufted sea pinks.

Then, all of a sudden, a few of the older cows made a sprinting beeline for the land as the incoming tide began to cover the white sand. Soon it was a mass rodeo stampede, cows and calves alike making an obviously well-rehearsed crossing before their link with the mainland was severed. With the connecting strand now gone, there was nothing for it but to remove shoes, roll up trouser legs and wade back through the swirl of warm water, now rather less inviting than before, for the incoming flow had dissolved the abundant cow pats, staining the water the colour of well-masked tea.

Above all the splashing, the echo of a distant cuckoo carried over the sea from Skye, and the air really was rent, not by the thunderclaps of the song, but by the banshee wailing of a pair of black-throated divers on the sea. Over on the island, a territorial sandpiper bobbed and chattered nervously from a shore rock, but it could have spared itself all its peeping, for the floodtide had restored the island solitude once more.

Deer days

JUNE is the time of the red deer's calving, when the fruits of the stag's labours in acquiring and fighting for his harem in the autumn rut appear on the open hillsides. Protected by nature from hill fox and golden eagle by its spotted coat, the newly born deer calf lies still and unmoving in the vegetation, visited by his mother for regular feeding. These days of deer ranging over bleak hillsides are a comparatively modern phenomenon, for the red deer is a beast of forest lands by right, forced to make a living on the open hills through destruction of the native woodland in earlier times and discouragement by custodians of the new generation of forests.

Although we tend to think of deer as distant creatures, even in summer days there are places where I see them close to busy roads, but to come over a ridge on a hill walk and all but touch some resting deer lying on the other side is one of the remembered pleasures of summer on the high hills.

Not long ago I took the opportunity to view Landseer's *Monarch of the Glen* when it was on view in Aberdeen Art Gallery. Seeing the painting in the flesh certainly gave a fresh perspective on this over-reproduced picture. Apart from the sheer power of body form with which the artist imbued his subject, the most intriguing thing to me was how brilliantly Landseer achieved the glistening wet nose effect by just the merest touch of white paint.

Sika deer I chance upon occasionally on summer days, especially in one Ross-shire strath where an open cover of birch and pine above the river seems to suit their needs. Introduced into Highland sporting estates from the Orient, Sika resemble red deer in many ways, though smaller in build. Such is the similarity between the two species that they're often hard to tell apart, and to make matters worse, they're also not averse to interbreeding, a matter of concern for the purity of native red deer stocks.

On Forvie Moor

THE start of June is a time when wildfowl broods are still appearing out of nowhere. It's then that I most enjoy a visit to the vast spread of sandblown land that is the Moor of Forvie north of Aberdeen, home to Scotland's largest colony of eider ducks, or dunters, to give them their northern name. Many a time I've all but trodden on an incubating female eider, her well-camouflaged body flattened protectively against heather or bent grass. More nervous birds take to the air with a heart-stopping clatter, showering nest and eggs with a foul-smelling stream of guano, just to put fox or stoat off the idea that they'd chanced upon a tasty meal. Eider nests are warm beds of finest breast down, a commodity once prized by self-sufficient northland folk who valued it long before duvets became the fashion.

After all the fervent ooing and cooing of their offshore courtship, large numbers of eider drakes take themselves off on a bachelors'

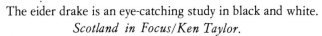

The eider drake is an eye-catching study in black and white.
Scotland in Focus/Ken Taylor.

outing down to the mouth of the Tay to loaf around and moult out their breeding plumage of black and white body and almond green nape, leaving their mates to cope with the trials of bringing up a family.

There's a wonderful synchronisation in the mass break-out of the baby eiders. One day the water's edge is devoid of young, the next there are masses of newly-hatched fluffy ducklings pattering everywhere, having been led through all the pitfalls of the rough terrain to the shallows of the shore. Individual claims to a particular brood are soon set aside, and creches of delinquent ducklings quickly form, shepherded along by matronly mothers and homely 'auntie' ducks in a glorious mixter-maxter of families.

Centuries ago, the great shifting sand dunes emptied themselves across Forvie village and its surrounding farmland. Ruin followed for the folk, who now have only the walls of the kirk as their memorial on the windswept face of the moor. Now it's an atmospheric place of sea winds and lonely spaces, of sand and silence and is designated the Sands of Forvie National Nature Reserve.

Once, I took some school pupils to the moor to view its wildlife. As we headed from the Ythan estuary towards the sea cliffs, the sky had taken on a queer look. Lowering black clouds were gathering all around, and beyond the farmlands of the Garioch, the Mither Tap of Bennachie had an uncommon blackness about it. It would have been the ideal setting for some supernatural happening, and, in a way, it turned out to be something like it. As we crossed the moor, a kestrel rose from the path, dropping its prey as it went. A few of the girls hurried forward, wide-eyed at the sight of a headless frog corpse, the empty socket a gory tribute to the kestrel's skills in the art of amphibian decapitation. Suddenly a chorus of skirling quines pierced the air. As they crowded round about, the headless corpse had lurched crazily forward in some delayed reflex action, a bizarre contribution to the moor's black mood that day.

Vanishing verges

JUNE is the month for colourful roadside verges, a vanishing and much undervalued part of our country scene. When spared the spraying and clinical shaving that are all too often their lot, there can be such a flowering in this linear no-man's land as to brighten many an otherwise tedious drive. Red and white campion, yellow-centred white gowans on elegant stems, and the ubiquitous scarlet poppy flourish along the verges, and I never tire of stopping to admire them against a backcloth of overgrown dyke or stone-faced bridge.

On a turf-capped sandstone dyke I know, curling ferns and scuttling lizards provide the backcloth to a verge that's filled with fresh-leaved wild raspberry canes and tall white umbellifers. 'Thunder flooers' we called them in childhood days, watching with horror as some big loon tempted us by decapitating them with a stick, for to damage one, we believed, was as certain a way to induce dreaded thunder as squashing a spider was of bringing on the rain.

Caucasian giants and mappie mous

FORTUNATELY, perhaps, as boys we didn't have the temptation of felling the great white-flowered stalks of the giant hogweed. Nowadays, this Caucasian garden escapee is a widespread plant in river valleys of the North-east where District Councils do battle with the towering giants for, in certain circumstances, the juice contained in the towering hollow stems can cause a severe skin irritation.

Looking around our Scottish country places at this early summer season, it's obvious that several foreign species are quite settled in. Another of the successes in the great plant escape story is the Himalayan balsam which flourishes along river banks and damp verges. Above its tall stems open the pink and white flowers that give it the name of policeman's helmet in southerly places where bobbies sport more balsam-like headgear.

A familiar plant of summer ditches in the lowlands is the bright yellow mimulus or monkey flower, another far-travelled immigrant. The coastlands of Western North America are its true abode, but it seems just as much at home along any Scottish burn as against the mountain backcloth of Alaska. Mimulus it may be by name to the botanist, but I knew it first as 'mappie mouie', like some other plants in the Scottish countryside named for its supposed resemblance to a rabbit's mouth. Another mappie mou escapee is the garden antirrhinum which can be seen brightening the face of the dark volcanic rocks on the Fife approaches to the Forth road bridge.

Prints from the past

FOSSILS have a fascination for most folk. It has something to do with the mystery that surrounds the life and times of creatures preserved from the past in their stony time-capsules. The shore is probably the best place to begin a fossil hunt, especially in the Old Red Sandstone and Carboniferous rocks which have been laid bare by the tides at many spots along the east coast. The black Jurassic shales of the Eathie cliff-foot in the Black Isle are peppered with the white coiled whorls of ammonites that once propelled themselves through ancient seas. But more fascinating by far are the fossils which the great nineteenth-century naturalist Hugh Miller extricated from the adjacent fish beds, exciting the emerging geological world of the time. Some of his finds are preserved in the little thatched cottage of his birth in Cromarty, a place well worth a summer visit. At Barnsness on the East Lothian coast there are abundant fossils in the limestone that once supplied the old lime kilns, and a wave-cut platform of a strange creamy colour, pitted with basin-shaped depressions.

But the seashore doesn't have a monopoly of fossils. In Glasgow's Victoria Park, the city has the good fortune to have its world-famous fossil grove, giving visitors a fascinating reminder of plants from the past in the remains of its ancient Carboniferous trees.

Native nostalgia

JUNE is the month of Scotland's premier agricultural show, when the farming countryside moves for a few days to the Royal Highland Showground at Ingliston outside Edinburgh. At this and all the other smaller agricultural society shows dotted around the country comes an opportunity for a sometimes nostalgic view of our native cattle scene. I was reared in Shorthorn country, enjoying the sight of well-fleshed white, red and roan beasts munching among the buttercups of their summer meadows. It was a white Shorthorn bull crossed with a Galloway cow that gave the distinctive 'blue-grey coo' once so beloved of Scottish farmers. But now, after the heady days of the Perth bull sales of the 1950s, when prizewinners fetched a fortune from Argentinian breeders, the breed has fallen on leaner times.

The sleek black Aberdeen Angus is the epitome of fine beef breeding, but, like the Shorthorn, has seen better days. Long gone are the summer parks filled with tail-swishing 'blacks' on the rolling plains of Aberdeenshire and the Mearns, their place taken now by peelie-wally Charolais beasts, hefty brown and white Simmental and lanky Limousin crosses, the progeny of Continental incomers favoured by a modern generation of farmers who point to profit margins as justification for replacing the handiwork of their forebears with such foreign incomers.

The hardy Galloway from the hill lands of the South-west is a link with the ancient black breeds of Western Europe, and has always found a niche in its native heartland. The appearance of its white-belted cousin at a show is always one of the most popular sights, for this is Scotland's representative of the 'sheeted cattle' of olden times. A herd of 'belties' is a rare sight indeed, but one which I used to enjoy in windswept fields overlooking the red granite cliffs of Buchan, a location diametrically the opposite of its South-western homeland.

Shetland cattle, a small dual-purpose black and white breed, are sadly diminished in the island scene. Nearly thirty years ago I remember a fine Shetland bull on Fair Isle which grew so fat on its rich island grazings that it became much too big for the boat to return it to its owners, for bulls have traditionally been put out on hire to island places.

Scotland's world-famous dairy breed, the rich brown and white Ayrshire, has also been losing ground, this time to the black and white Friesian and Holstein, so I relish a journey through its western homeland for the sight of so many fine beasts still contentedly chewing their cud in the lush rolling pastures of the west.

Black-throated divers and gold-eared grebes

THE Highland landscape is dotted with lochs where eerie-wailing black-throated and red-throated divers make their summer homes. The sight and sound of a black-throated diver are so evocative of the wild Highlands that I view with concern the continued ill fortunes of this magnificent bird. Sadly, breeding black-throats are not doing well, with fluctuating water levels, unthinking fishermen and visitors, and despicable egg collectors who come from the south to pillage our rare bird riches. There's some hope, though, that a few may choose to

Slavonian grebe, the golden-eared treasure of Highland lochs.
Scotland in Focus/Laurie Campbell.

nest on the special nesting platforms created for them on some of our northern lochs. These rise and fall with the changing water levels, providing a more reliable nest site for this expert swimmer whose legs are positioned so far behind its body that life on land is almost impossible to cope with.

But perhaps the brightest gem of the Highland summer is the Slavonian grebe with its golden ear tufts and deep red plumage. At Loch Ruthven in Inverness-shire there's now a superb opportunity to see this rare bird of the Highland lochs from a waterside hide. Somewhat outwith its normal province, the Slavonian grebe has nested at the Loch of the Lowes near Dunkeld, but its reed-fringed waters are more favoured by great-crested grebes. At lowland water bodies like the Loch of Kinnordy near Kirriemuir, grebes again catch the eye, for dabchick and great-crested are both present.

Exotic strangers

THE most surprising event at the Loch of Kinnordy in recent years has been the arrival of the North American ruddy-duck, a cocky little escapologist which has decided to adopt our countryside. The Oriental mandarin duck is another escapee well settled in Britain, though mostly furth of Scotland. By the side of the fast-flowing waters of the Tay at Perth may seem an unlikely setting for such an exotic creature as the Mandarin, but it's there that I like to scan the banks in search of one of the flamboyant drakes from the small local population. By this time of year they need more looking for, though, as the drakes are exchanging their showy orange plumes and erect wing sails for the more dowdy plumage of their consorts. This home setting with its rod-casting fishers and grey town buildings really does seem a hemisphere away from the landscape with rice fields and pagodas where I thrilled once to the sight of wild Mandarins at a wooded pool on the Japanese island of Honshu.

In our well-managed lowland landscape, surviving patches of marsh and bog provide a last link with the wetland wildernesses which once marked the low-lying areas. Among their sprouting rushes and waving reeds, you can come as close to wild nature in a lowland setting as it's possible to be. On the long June evenings, the harsh cries of water hen echo from the hidden depths of reedbeds where sedge warblers scrape their summer song, an outpouring in which the poet Edward Thomas heard

> '. . . the small brown birds
> Wisely reiterating endlessly
> What no man learnt yet, in or out of school.'

Possil Marsh is a place where some feeling of wetland wilderness may still be sensed, albeit on a small scale, just beyond the urban sprawl of Glasgow. Among its reed beds and willow scrub, grasshopper warblers sometimes add their own strange song to that of their small brown cousins, with a sound that suggests an angler reeling in his line.

Lochwinnoch likewise is a marshland place accessible to the urban areas of Strathclyde, with opportunities for enjoying the riches of wetland wildlife, and the added bonus of being able to oversee the whole panorama from its observation tower. On the more open water, shovelers shovel with spatulate beaks along the muddy margins, while great-crested grebes, the crowning glory of the reserve, perform their strangely neck-stretching and dancing routines. With the contribution of the curious 'drumming' of snipe in their display flights, the Lochwinnoch marshlands resound to a varied collection of sounds once widespread before drainage robbed the land of so much of its wildlife interest.

JULY

'The cry o' a whaup at the watter-mou',
An' the smell o' tangle-bree;
The whisper o' win' throu' quiverin' girss,
An' the low saft sang o' the sea.'

PETER BUCHAN

*J*ULY is a month to enjoy nature's bounty in the days of high summer. Though I live now by the sea, I still think of July as a holiday month of trips to the beach and walks by the shore. In the climatic happenings that determine whether we have a real Scottish summer or not, the pressure patterns over a remote set of Atlantic islands play a key role, so if the weather chart promises an anticyclone over the Azores, I can savour the thought of sunny seaside days to set fritillaries fluttering and dolphins displaying.

Where dolphins delight

THE delicately-patterned brown fritillaries are still common enough butterflies on grassy seaside cliffs, but the bottle-nosed dolphins which once were a widespread part of the coastal scene are now sadly uncommon. As an island race, we've not dealt kindly with our dolphin neighbours, upsetting their coastal environment. Fortunately, we still have one remaining group of reasonable size, its lively members inhabiting the waters of the Inner Moray Firth, where they often stage a show that leaves seaworld circus acts well and truly in the shade.

I'm fortunate in living close to Chanonry Ness on the Black Isle, for the tip of this small peninsula within a peninsula is now possibly the best vantage point for dolphin-watching around our entire coastline. On July's long evenings, when daylight fades to an orange glow behind the outlined western hills, dark-finned shapes surface beneath the forbidding ramparts of Fort George. At times they rise singly, but more often in unison, when their steamy blowing carries on the evening air. The dolphins, young and old alike, really do have a whale of a time, leaping straight out of the water and returning nose-first in graceful arcs. Sometimes they perform a half-turn before hitting the surface with an almighty crack of their streamlined bodies. When the river-seeking salmon are running up the firth, it's exhilarating to watch the dolphins in the maelstrom of churning water at the Point, working closely together, then suddenly breaking pack out of the tide-rip, making the fish leap out of the water before them in sheer panic.

Island going

HOLIDAY times are an opportunity really to enjoy the living Scottish scene, and what better way than to take a summer sail among the scattered islands of the Inner Hebrides. One of my most unforgettable island trips began on a morning of settled calm at the start of July as I sailed out of Oban on the *Columba*, bound for the island of Tiree. Shortly afterwards, this ageing servant of the Caledonian MacBrayne fleet was to be removed, Cinderella-like, from the humdrum of island service and transformed into the glamour role of Hebridean cruise ship. But for the moment the red-funnelled vessel was pursuing more mundane duties, nosing her well-practised way out of harbour and past the green Isle of Lismore. The early morning sea was a glassy calm, broken only by guillemots, razorbills and puffins plopping into the green depths at the ship's approach, a trace of air bubbles marking their descent.

On the water all around, lines of stiff-winged Manx shearwaters planed effortlessly across a waveless Sound of Mull, the scree-covered slopes of their nesting haunts on distant Rhum just catching the early sun. It put me in mind of an earlier July day, trudging up those self-same slopes of Hallival, named by the Vikings and claimed by nesting shearwaters, admiring the scattered island scene, but appreciating much more the escape from the clegs that had so mercilessly savaged my legs at lowland Kinloch where sturdy Rhum ponies grazed.

Now a wealth of other Hebridean isles floated mirage-like above the horizon: flat-topped Lunga and Fladda of the Treshnish Isles;

unpretentious Canna; Eigg with its rocky Sgurr. On the surface calm
sat Bac Mor, the Dutchman's Cap, strange-shaped survivor from an
ancient age when volcanoes spluttered out the fiery contents of their
magma chambers. And in prominent outline, Sgeir na h'Iolaire, the
Eagle's Crag, where ernes once sat, and may sit again, for the majestic
sea eagle has been reintroduced from Norway and soars once more
above ancient Hebridean strongholds.

As the ship's engines died to a gentle throb outside Coll's little
pier, two sleek pairs of black-throated divers rippled the calm, while a
pale-plumaged Arctic skua ventured a closer look at the commotion
which the arrival of an island steamer brings. Soon we had cast off
again, heading this time for distant Tiree — 'a landscape of houses', as
someone appropriately described it. It's certainly the homes of the
people — some still freshly thatched in muran, the seaside bent grass
— that are the most striking features as you approach this low-lying,
sandy isle.

As the *Columba* lightened its load of passengers and assorted
freight at the pier, a few white-topped Atlantic breakers spent
themselves along the line of Gott Bay, its white crescent beach
cradling waters of sky-reflecting blue. Along the shore, I paused to
listen to a soaring skylark above flat green machair that was studded
pink with yarrow and permeated by the warm scent of clovers. Some
whaups bubbled and curlewed their lonely calls beyond the level
sward, and a passing black-tailed godwit lifted lankily from the water's
edge. Crossing the machair was like walking over a scented carpet,
with its profusion of pink orchids, spreading mauve mats of aromatic
thyme, and delicate pale yellow flowers of meadow rue gently nodding
above feathered green foliage. Here was the Hebridean scene at its
best: a living potpourri of summer scents drawn out by the warmth
and backed by evocative island sounds.

Pirates of the northern sea skies

SCOTLAND is a land of islands, with distinctive personalities that
make each a pleasure to know. I recall other July days, spent among
the Northern Isles with their legacy of a Viking past. Fair Isle is the
Fridarey of the Norsemen, a great sea-girt rock halfway between
Orkney and Shetland, where skuas mercilessly dive-bomb intruders

Bonxie on a northern island moor — a practised master of menace.
Scotland in Focus/Laurie Campbell.

who violate their airspace or rashly cross the invisible bounds of their nesting territory. To the Shetlanders, the swift-flying Arctic skuas are 'skootie allens' and their bulky great skua cousins are 'bonxies'. Both are skilled in the art of harassment, shamelessly pursuing terns and forcing them to surrender their hard-won catches of fish.

From a distance, a boorach of bonxies on an island moor has the look of a homely gathering of farmyard hens, but there the similarity definitely ends. Once on the wing, bonxies are masters of menace, striking terror into unsuspecting intruders, be they ovine, bovine or human, for sheep, cattle and people receive the same treatment. Somehow I suspect that when Hitchcock was seeking a location for filming *The Birds* he wasn't aware of the skua colonies of Shetland.

Fair Isle has an excellent accommodation centre at its bird observatory, founded after the war by George Waterston, the much-respected Edinburgh ornithologist. As it's a place of pilgrimage for birdwatchers from all over the world, it was no surprise on the island one early July day to find an American lady birdwatcher arriving off the little island mailboat. She was clearly determined to waste no time in seeing the different birds of another continent, for the next morning she was early on the go, binoculars and camera round neck and red knitted hat on head. Not long afterwards, while cycling past the moor that flanks the island's road, my eye was drawn to some noisy stramash among the skuas. A strange-looking shape on the ground was being dive-bombed by a particularly noisy and intimidating pair of bonxies. From a distance the object of their ire looked like some gigantic caterpillar, ungainly body arched in the middle as it shuffled slowly across the heather, only, this caterpillar was sporting a bright red toorie! The American lady had found her different birds all right, but the Fair Isle bonxies had turned out to be rather more different than she'd bargained for.

Outwith their breeding grounds, it's worth watching for the early skua migration down the east coast, for they winter far to the south of their Viking summer isles. Any headland will do, and with binoculars and patience, their dark forms can be seen flighting southwards . . . taking time off here and there to practise a bit of extortion on the side, of course.

Observing ospreys

OSPREYS are also summer visitors and also depend on a diet of fish, but the skuas' piratical ways contrast with the fish hawk's more direct approach, snatching live prey out of the water. Speyside is probably still the best place for seeing a Scottish osprey, since it's at the Loch Garten site near Boat of Garten that these magnificent birds of prey have nested for the past three decades, thanks to the RSPB's Operation Osprey.

More than once I've had an early morning road journey from Inverness to Perth rewarded by the sight of an osprey fishing on the river at Aviemore, long before the holiday village had begun to stir. Not far away is pine-fringed Loch an Eilean where some of the last ospreys were harried and robbed in earlier days. The crumbling castle ruins on which the birds made their eyrie can still be seen today. After

Osprey at its summer Highland eyrie. *Scotland in Focus/Roger Wilson.*

their extermination, Speyside was recolonised by Scandinavian ospreys. Some time later a pair obligingly nested at the Scottish Wildlife Trust reserve at the Loch of the Lowes in Perthshire. Now dozens of Scottish-bred youngsters are being reared in eyries all over the north, so it's worth looking out in summer for fishing ospreys at such places as Findhorn Bay on the Moray Coast, the shallows of the Cromarty Firth, and across the Moray Firth in the tidal waters of the Kyles of Sutherland.

Having been involved in Operation Osprey in its earliest days, I still associate the bird most strongly with the valley of the Spey, but sightings elsewhere in Scotland are increasing, and when the birds disperse towards their African wintering grounds, they can now turn up almost anywhere. The osprey is a distinctive bird with brown and white body pattern, and characteristic hovering while trying to spot a fish lying close to the surface. With a sudden splash, the powerful talons descend like bolts from the blue to latch on to the back of a luckless pike or trout or even a flatfish, depending on the locale.

A still and midge-infested July evening by pine-enclosed Loch Garten provided my closest encounter with a fishing osprey. Beyond the floating green pads and open white cups of the water lilies, an osprey came in to fish not far from shore. After quartering the placid water for a time, the hunter suddenly dropped, emerging with a good-sized catch whose writhings reflected the evening sun. With a shake of his feathers and a cascade of water droplets above still-spreading ripples, the silent fisher departed, winging his way in the direction of the eyrie tree and a hungry mate, fish pointed head into wind.

Perhaps one day we'll see Scottish osprey eyries high on the tops of electricity pylons, as I remember one along the forested valley of the Glomma River in southern Norway. With so many volts passing along the cables below, these Nordic ospreys were definitely into self-help schemes, taking advantage of the ultimate in anti-theft devices.

Goosanders and grey wagtails

IT'S a source of shame that Scottish ospreys were so ruthlessly persecuted last century for the crime of taking fish from rivers and lochs. It was a fate shared with the goosander, that attractive saw-billed duck of Scottish river systems, which even now is still heavily shot along waters like the Tweed. The goosander is surely one of the classic Scottish birds, for the drake is a wildfowl of rare beauty with his bottle-green head, red bill and pink-tinged cream body feathering. By July, the new crop of ducklings have mostly tumbled out of their lofty nest-holes in riverside trees and taken to the fast-flowing waters. But there are some quite public spots where goosanders may be more easily seen, like the old Telford bridge at Dunkeld where I've watched drakes diving in the rushing waters of the Tay, and beside the old railway bridge at Inverness before it was swept into the Ness in the 1989 spate.

Goosanders share their summer homes with another bird of swift-flowing rivers and burns. The grey wagtail's name understates its true appearance, a pleasing medley of slate grey and canary yellow. It's a bird I never tire of watching, associating it in my mind (like the dipper) with the rushing of a burn over water-worn stones, or the plashing waters of a mill lade. Unhappily, mill lades are few and far between these days as meal mills have closed and their water wheels crumbled away, but on an otherwise depressing July day of low cloud and swirling Highland smoor, I was cheered by the sight of a grey wagtail happily feeding its young right beside the turning water wheel of the old mill at Blair Atholl, only feet removed from visitors coming and going from the mill coffee shop above.

Legless lizards

WHERE might you find a legless lizard? The answer isn't outside a pub, but on open rough ground on summer days, for the reptilean slow worm just happens to be a lizard that's dispensed with its legs. Slow worms are harmless, dark-coloured creatures of the summer countryside, slithering their way through the undergrowth in the manner of snakes, resulting in some unjustifiable persecution. Slow worms tend not to bask as much as adders, but on summer days I sometimes come upon them wriggling their way along verge and forest edge.

Their common lizard cousins I see far more frequently, especially when days are fine and there's sunshine to be soaked up. Like the dinosaurs of old, lizards need the warmth of the sun to get themselves going. I've come upon them in a springtime torpor, safely hidden beneath a stone, awaiting a rise in the air temperature outside. It's best not to try to handle these native reptiles, for they have the disconcerning habit of leaving their tails behind, or at least a goodly proportion of them, as they make a slippery bid for freedom.

Lizards are widespread on moors and along grassy banks and drystone dykes, but must be decidedly uncommon in bedrooms. Yet, on entering our bedroom one warm and sunny day in June, I found one scuttling under the bed. It had clearly been sunning itself on the window sill and for some reason had decided to go walkabout inside.

Summer days see the tiny young born into a world of threatening bird beaks, for a baby lizard makes a tasty morsel. The new generation is born alive, not hatched from incubated clutches of eggs, and the perfect miniature charm of a baby lizard is hard to describe. On sunny days I've sometimes watched little ones dart about on a favourite basking place — a heap of discarded old wood and rusting corrugated iron which was clearly to the lizards' liking as a warmth-absorbing place.

Summer on the high hills

SUMMER days are special days among the high hills. Where eagles plane over ice-gouged corrie bowls, the world of the sub-Arctic prevails. Here is the high summer home of the dotterel, that most gentle of waders, so confiding that folk once thought it a foolish creature, hence its name. Perhaps nothing expresses better the wild spirit of the summer mountain scene than the sight of a little 'trip' of dotterel flighting in the silence of some high plateau.

Since the 1950s the Arctic connection has been reinforced on the Cairngorms by the presence of a herd of reindeer. Introduced from Sweden by the Lapp, Mikel Utsi, they roam the high tops, browsing on Cladonia, the reindeer 'moss', and whatever other lichens their high level pastures can provide.

On the high plateaux, green alpine club moss springs impressively from bare peat spreads, and 'lousy loorie' (properly *Loiseleuria procumbens*, the mountain azalea), brightens its prostrate mats with small pink flowers. Somehow I never cease to be surprised at coming upon the thrift and roseroot at such lofty elevations, for they seem so much a part of the seaside plant scene. But my favourite of all Scottish alpines is the pink-flowered moss campion which spreads its moss-like green mats across the weathered rock.

Any gardener with a penchant for alpines will tell you that lime-rich soils are loved by so many of the choice plants. And so it is on our Highland mountains, where lime-enriched flushes provide ideal growing places for rare beauties. Perhaps because it reminds me so much of glorious days spent in high mountain meadows abroad, our rare indigenous blue spring gentian is a particular favourite. Glen Clova and Caenlochan in the heart of the Grampians have a reputation for rare alpines, but Ben Lawers in Perthshire has long drawn visitors to view its superb mountain flora, guided by the National Trust for Scotland whose particular interest the mountain's alpine flora has been.

Moss campion spreads its mossy green mats over high mountain plateaux. *Douglas Willis.*

Pine trees tower above Culbin's dunes in Scotland's vanished desert. *Douglas Willis.*

Trees in the desert

THE notion of trees in a desert may conjure up a vision of waving palms around an oasis, but Scotland's own desert really did once exist, and trees were the cause of its disappearing act.

Until the mass afforestation of the drifting dunes, the Culbin Sands on the Moray Firth formed a vast tract of fine sand, readily whipped into dust storms by the winds that blew unchecked across its lonely wilderness. So great a resemblance was there to the dry desert lands to the east that when an unprecedented immigration of Pallas's sand grouse took place into Western Europe in the 1880s, a few actually settled down to breed among the dunes. Sadly, these rarest of Scottish birds soon fell foul of the gunsmen and taxidermists, for it was the age when everything unusual had to be bagged, following the maxim that 'What's hit is history and what's missed is mystery!'

But the Culbin Sands concealed a human tragedy, too. 'Here lay a fair fat land,' wrote the poet Andrew Young, for this was once a fertile place of bountiful harvests. The tragic story of Culbin's shifting sands reached its dramatic conclusion in a great storm in the seventeenth century when the well-tilled Barony lands disappeared for ever beneath a suffocating blanket of sand. Mindful of the ruin of Culbin's laird, later generations of landowners began a tree-planting programme along the fringes.

With the advent of the Forestry Commission came the total transformation of this most distinctive part of the Scottish scene, as dunes were thatched with brushwood and Scots pine planted into the sandy ground. Today there remains no trace of the vanished community of Culbin, but I like to walk alone among its tall maturing pines, for it's an atmospheric place where the ghosts of the past find voice in the soughing of the sea wind.

Now the Culbin Forest has taken on a strong resemblance to the old Caledonian pine forest of the hinterland. Wintergreen and creeping lady's tresses spring from the needle carpet, just as they do in the old pine stands, while capercaillie, crossbill and crested tit complete the picture of a native pinewood community. I never come away from Culbin without some bonus, perhaps the sight of bright-eyed roe deer observing my presence with uncertainty before bounding off among the old dunes, or the fluttering presence of a dark Scots argus butterfly accompanying me on my walk along a forest ride, or the green sheen and bright red wing markings of a six-spot burnet moth as it settles on a mauve mat of flowering thyme.

Toads in trouble

IN *The Wind in the Willows*, Mr Toad was possessed of a great knowledge. But the accumulated amphibian wisdom of the ages isn't always passed on to each new generation of toadlets, it seems. I came to this conclusion one hot July day along the Black Isle shore where a seaward-flowing burn was impounded by a shingle bar. As I approached, something about the small pool took my eye. The surface seemed to be in a turmoil. A moving black shape was rippling the water.

Closer inspection revealed a quivering black mass of toadlets, some in the process of making the metamorphosis from water-based tadpole to land-based toad. But then the story took a gruesome twist. Some of the more adventurous toadlets had already left the water and crawled on to the stones at the edge of the pool. The trouble was that the stones were burning hot and the toads were literally baking before my eyes. Many had already perished, stuck fast to the blistering surface, but the others continued to press on, lemming-like, towards this macabre suicide.

So adolescent toads maybe aren't so bright. But there's a haughtiness about a warty adult as he sits and glares impassively at you from a grassy tussock. Distasteful secretions from its body make the toad unpalatable to many predators, but many perish on the roads while moving towards a favoured spawning pond. It's a phenomenon I had cause to curse late one evening when in a hurry back from the West Coast. The road was alive with crossing toads, making driving a real trial as I did my best to avoid them. Many, alas, had fallen victim to unthinking or uncaring drivers. Toads will definitely not be hurried. They amble their way through life, taking great long strides when negotiating obstructions on the way, unlike the more streamlined puddock which prefers a louping lifestyle.

Summer quails and rasping rails

JULY isn't noted for its birdsong, but there's an uncommon one that's worth listening for. Scotland is just a bit far north of the quail's preferred range, but in recent times we seem to have been lucky in having a few of these diminutive game birds calling in our part of the country. It's a sound to listen to on long summer evenings when the air is still and the trisyllabic *quic, quic-ic* travels a surprising distance. Supposedly sounding like 'wet my lips' to the human ear, the calling seems to come from one corner of a field one minute, the opposite corner the next.

Ventriloquist acts were a speciality also of the corncrake in the days before farming became so mechanised. The advent of modern hay-cutting methods was bad news for this land rail which had nested all over the farmlands of Scotland, *crek-crekking* monotonously into the night air. Other factors also seem to have played their part in the sad decline of this distinctive ground-nester, but the fact is that only where hay-cutting is less mechanised and where large-scale drainage has spared the flag iris beds which they like, do a few corncrakes still return each summer to the crofting lands of the west to utter their rasping lovesong, and help recall an earlier age when farming was more of a manual art than the mechanised process it has become today.

Among such last places are the green isles of the Inner Hebrides, and it was there that I recently enjoyed lying in bed with the window wide open, listening to the lovesong of the crakes filling the night air, and pleasantly recalling departed island days. My July countryside memories are haunted by that repetitive sound: memories of the stillness of a Shetland clifftop in the midnight light of the simmer dim, as a distant corncrake rasped against a background of churring guillemots below, willing their youngsters to take that first brave tumble into the dark abyss of the night; of lying on my stomach, parting the waving stalks of ripening bere on a North Ronaldsay croft, and having an unnerving eyeball-to-eyeball encounter with the corncrake tenant; of a pocket of green croftland among the grey rock outcrops near Scourie where the old crofter wife had put up a sign proclaiming that a hurriedly scythed corner of her hayfield had been declared a 'CAMPING SIGHT' and that you could enjoy the privilege of pitching your tent there for half a crown. I suppose for the price we couldn't have expected much more, but muttering something about the 'faceelities', the cailleach gave a toothless grin and waved vaguely in the direction of a nearby flag iris bed. What she omitted to add was that these particular flags of convenience were already occupied by corncrakes. And she maintained a discreet silence on the matter of the dawn corncrake corroboree with its barrage of loud rasping, against which the canvas of our little tent could offer no defence.

There's still time — just — to indulge in the nostalgia of hearing this countryside sound from the past, but it usually means taking a boat for the pleasure. Though for those who have had to thole sleepless corncrake nights, I suspect that this might not be everybody's word to describe this particular Scottish countryside experience!

AUGUST

*A*UGUST can be a real dual-personality month. When the weather is sunny it has that satisfying feel of real high summer, disguising the already fading freshness of country places. But when the Atlantic depressions take a more southerly track and bring their rain fronts with them, the best that can be hoped for is that there will be some glowing September days to follow.

Butterfly days

GIVEN a sunny spell, though, August days of swelling fruit and seeding grasses may be good butterfly days as well. I'm greatly attracted by painted ladies, though for reputation's sake, it might be as well to

Mauve-flowering panicles of buddleia are irresistible to the painted lady butterfly. *Douglas Willis.*

stress that I have in mind those lovely Mediterranean insects which sometimes grace our garden, resplendent in yellowish-orange markings with white wing tips.

On occasion we've seen dozens of them with the more familiar tortoiseshells on the flowering mauve panicles of buddleia. If there's room in the garden to allow it a reasonable spread, then this Chinese butterfly bush is a must for its happy combination of attractiveness and conservation value. In a great seasonal outburst it seeds itself shamelessly around, so that young plants are easily come by. Garden centres stock other forms, too, from white to deepest purple, like the really dark 'Black Knight'.

Red admirals also arrive from the south at this time and are often confused with the more orange-coloured tortoiseshell, but with its bright markings of red, white and black there's really no mistaking this aristocrat among garden butterflies. Red admirals are also surprisingly territorial, taking the same route each time through the garden on their fluttering excursions, and sunning themselves in the same spots each day.

The Glorious Twelfth

I'VE never really appreciated why the twelfth of the month should be described as 'glorious', for it's a day of blasting guns and plummeting grouse bodies over northern moors. Although the red grouse's scientific name is *Lagopus lagopus scoticus*, the Scottish crossbill of the old Highland pinewoods really has a better claim to being the country's national bird, since it doesn't find life south of the Border to its taste at all. But it hasn't had the huge media hype of the grouse, extolling the virtues of a particular brand of uisge-beatha, or featuring in the hoo-ha over which posh London hotel can produce the first Scottish grouse for breakfast.

A curious feature of the grouse story is that its populations build up, only to crash as disease takes its toll, so measures are now taken to reduce the death rate by leaving out medicated grit on their heather-clad moors. For the grouse, it's clearly not a spoonful of sugar that makes the medicine go down, but rather a good shovelful of gravel!

Dressed to kill

AT the parade of Highland ponies at our local Black Isle Farmers' Show, held in the first week of August, there's sometimes a garron with wicker basket panniers for bringing down the shot grouse from the hills. It's part of a tradition of inviting Highland gamekeepers and ghillies to parade with their hardy ponies, both clad in best hill gear. Accompanied by their masters in heavy tweeds, deerstalker hats and dangling brass telescopes, the brown and grey garrons parade round the ring with their harness and saddles for bringing down the dead stags from the hills. They're fine-looking beasts, and still with a job to do in the land that bred them — rough hill ground that demands all the stamina and sure-footedness in which they excel.

Till recent times, the diminutive Shetland pony also had a transport role. The Vikings would have ridden and worked shaggy little beasts such as these, and I once had a pleasant encounter with a crofter wife in wrap-over apron and 'tammie' on the Shetland island of Unst as she led her line of peat-laden ponies over from the peat banks to her home. Years ago, in less happy circumstances, I visited a small Rhondda Valley coal mine where Shelties still toiled for a living in the grimy underground darkness. Nowadays, this little islander has found a happier rôle as children's pony, adjusting well to conditions sometimes very different from those on its windswept island home.

Bonny blooming heather

BY the time the guns and hip flasks are out, the heather moors are coming into their seasonal purple bloom. In its late summer flowering, *Calluna vulgaris* brings character to the Highlands and cash to the Highlanders. Foreign visitors adore it, remove it by the handful from roadsides, drive away with great tufts sticking out of radiator grills, and generally use it to let everybody know that they've been to Scotland.

In days gone by, this was a useful plant around the home. The heather-thatched Leanach Cottage at Culloden battlefield is a reminder of days when a heather roof was a protection from the wet of a Highland winter. Archaeologists also remind us of the plant's use from earliest times. I like to think of those shadowy Stone Age folk who inhabited the subterranean housing estate of Skara Brae in Orkney, huddled together in their heather beds under that great midden heap, as storms lashed the Bay of Skaill outside.

At the Speyside Heather Centre at Skye of Curr near Carrbridge, David and Betty Lambie have created one of Speyside's visitor attractions in their colourful heather garden and nursery, where an interesting display now helps recall the plant's uses in the past.

Slithering adders

IT'S on open sunny tracks on heather moors that I've most often observed that zig-zag pattern as a basking adder slithers silently into the growth. It's said that its name derives from an Anglo-Saxon word which later became 'nadder', and 'a nadder' became 'an adder'. At any rate, it's certain that this much-maligned creature has declined since the days of the Anglo-Saxons, for it shuns cultivated places. At a popular stopping place on a scenic Highland road, a sign was erected exhorting visitors to 'Beware Adders'. Later, some wag felt moved to put up his own sign nearby. It read 'Beware Subtractors'! Perhaps it was the work of the same hand which, in recent times, has cleverly transformed the outline of a Cheviot sheep on some Highland road signs into that of an elephant, giving unwitting tourists some apprehension for the journey to come.

Goldfinches and thistles

APART from grouse, there's another characteristic harvest of the late summer moors. With hives and swarms removed to the hills in a vague echo of the old shieling movement of man and beast, bees that earlier buzzed among the yellow lowland squares of oilseed rape now toil to make their heather honey against a purple backcloth.

But August is a month of other wild harvests, too; of bursting seed heads, and of thistle tops tightly packed in silver-threaded down. This is one of the best times in the year for watching goldfinches tackle the thistle seed bonanza. Even now, I scarcely pass one by

The fiercely spiked spear thistle, symbol of Scotland's pride.
Scotland in Focus/Eric Middleton.

without putting my binoculars upon it, just to admire once more that marvellous pattern of crimson head and bright gold wing bars.

The goldfinch once paid a heavy price for its colourful feathering and cheery song. Trapped and caged by the thousand, it suffered a sad decline, but in this more enlightened age whole charms of goldfinches — sometimes a dozen at a time — are drawn to the brown heads of our buddleias, to search assiduously for the little brown seeds.

As they send the thistledown drifting on its way, I doubt if the goldfinches are pondering the question 'Which is the true Scotch thistle?' The spear thistle is perhaps the favourite candidate, with its proud flower heads and fierce 'Wha daur meddle wi me?' spikes. This was probably what Burns knew as the 'burr thistle', acknowledging its symbolism when he wrote:

> 'I turn'd the weeder-clips aside
> And spar'd the symbol dear.'

The showy musk thistle also has a claim, while the nodding melancholy thistle which grows around the fringes of our hills was reputedly the badge of James I, though it's quite thornless, and hardly seems a manly enough emblem for a monarch.

Curiously enough, the one perhaps most often called the Scotch thistle isn't a native at all. It's the tall, silvery-grey candelabra plant that adorns the grounds of Holyrood Palace in Edinburgh. Legend has it that this, the cotton thistle, recalls places where Mary Queen of Scots tarried, and sprang up from seeds scattered by her maids. The whole thistle argument was recently summed up in a delightful little book, *The Thistles of Scotland*, from Glasgow Museums and Art Galleries.

Birds and birdies don't mix

'FREEDOM and whisky gang thegither' was the Bard's sage observation, but the same can't be said for golf and birdwatching — in my experience at any rate. On a recent visit with my son to the attractive little golf course at Gairloch in Wester Ross, he was the golfer, I the passive admirer of the mid-August scene.

Beyond the outcropping red Torridonian Sandstone of the mainland edge, and backed by the distant grey outline of the Long

White-plumaged gannets crowd the volcanic slopes of the
Bass Rock. *Scotland in Focus/Ken Taylor.*

Island, a gannet was systematically quartering the cobalt waters of the
bay. Every now and again, the black-pointed wings would suddenly
fold as he dropped like a dart into the blue depths, an unlucky fish
halfway down his gullet by the time he'd surfaced.

The scene reminded me of why I no longer play golf. It has to do
with becoming preoccupied more with birds than with birdies, for my
golfing days were played out on an east-coast links course where the
August passage of gannets brought the birds really close inshore.
Sometimes their mass diving would be like a rain of white spears
among the scattering fish shoals, and my next shot up the fairway
would have to wait as I took in the sheer spectacle of it all. Interesting
migrant birds also had a distracting habit of hanging about the
fairways, so it was perhaps an inevitable progression to carrying a pair
of binoculars in my golf bag. This did not prove popular with my
partners, so in the interests of birdwatching, the golf was gradually
abandoned.

The Scottish links courses are good coastal birdwatching places,
but many spots down the east side have potential for observing the

passage of gannets and other seabirds as they leave their nesting grounds and head for more open waters. A car parking place with a seawards view makes a good vantage point for watching this annual dispersal. Adult gannets are easily identified by their brilliant white plumage and contrasting black wing tips. They also have a determined flight, but the mass dive-bombing is their most exciting feature, a sight I recall most vividly from the sea beneath the towering heights of the St Kildan cliffs. *Sula bassana*, the solan goose, recalls in its scientific name its long association with the Bass Rock in the Firth of Forth, a fascinating place which can be visited in summer by boat from North Berwick. And in a curiously matching setting, the volcanic rock-faces of Ailsa Craig in the Firth of Clyde are thronged with the white forms of nesting gannets.

With a taste and texture than only a Lewisman could love, young gannets, or gugas, are eagerly sought yet from the men of Ness in Lewis who yearly go in time-honoured fashion to the far-flung island of Sulisgeir to harvest this bounty of the western sea.

Return of the natives

A friend has a small fold of Highland cattle, this being the preferred term for a herd of these shaggy-coated animals. They're a great draw for tourists in their roadside field at this time of year, with their handlebar horns and cuddly calves. In summing up their character there can be no better quotation than from A. Gardiner of Dyce who described them as:

> 'The hairy horned heilan kye that gawk and glower the passer by'.

Their forebears were darker animals by far, invariably referred to as 'black' cattle in the accounts of the days of the men who walked them towards the trysts of Crieff and Stirling, then southwards along ancient drove roads. Some can still be traversed today, like the well-tramped Lairig Ghru and the Lairig an Laoigh (the calves' pass) from Speyside over into Deeside, and the track from Braemar to Blair Atholl through Glen Tilt, one of Scotland's great walks.

But now, after years of selective breeding the Highlander has come to be the reddish-coloured animal we're familiar with today.

Recently, though, black beasts have been appearing once more, and a fine contrast they make to their red-haired companions. Recognised for its ability to convert hill grazing into fine quality beef, the Highlander has travelled far from its native heath to places where its hardy attributes are recognised and valued. Here at home the natives have returned to many places, encouraged by the steady trade experienced in recent times at their annual sale in Oban. Fittingly enough, the food canning firm of Baxter's of Speyside, whose Highland produce goes all over the world, have established a fine fold of Highlanders in a magnificent setting by their Fochabers premises above the salmon-rich waters of the Spey.

Birds of a feather

AUGUST is a month when the old adage really takes on fresh meaning. Even as the month begins, the first autumn flocking has started. Round our way we see masses of pied wagtails bobbing and twittering on the short turf of our school playing field. Sometimes their numbers run into hundreds as they dart about over the short grass and feed among the very feet of the cattle in the surrounding fields, like egrets around grazing wildebeest in some African game park, rushing this way and that as lurking wee beasties are flushed from the pasture.

Now's the time to look out for the early flocking of lapwings in fields bordering roadsides, each year's gathering being a re-run of the one that went before. The start of the month brings a handful to favourite fields along our part of the firth, but by the end there are usually sixty or seventy birds passing between shore and field with their characteristic twinkling flight, hanging like black and white cut-outs in a mobile above the cliff updraught before dropping to the shore below.

On August days I sometimes see the greylag geese in the Strath of Kildonan in Sutherland. Not for them the long haul back from Iceland, but a life of laid-back loafing after summer days on nearby lochs. Yet, interesting though this summer goose-watching might be, the activities of the nearby gold panners can be infinitely more fascinating, as they wade into the flowing burn, swilling the water round and round in one kind of receptacle or another. Some bring proper shallow pans with them, like the 'Forty-niners' of old, while others make do with battered old frying pans with handles still attached. But it all serves the same purpose, and all are drawn to Baille an Or (town of the gold) with one shared hope: to chance upon the merest trace of the precious metal which once gave Scotland its own goldrush fever.

Where salmon loup

THE gold-panner's disappointment at the river in spate is the salmon fisher's dream come true. When heavy August rains turn mountain torrents to a peaty flow it's time to watch the salmon leap the falls. Using the pent-up force in their tails to hurl themselves into the wild torrents, the big fish head for the very heart of the crashing water; lithe, dark forms struggling against the downward flow. Sometimes they succeed, but often they retreat into the swirling brown depths, biding their time for one more try. It's a sight that has stirred the hearts of watchers for generations at the classic leaping places, like the Brig o Feugh on lower Royal Deeside, or the Falls of Shin near Lairg.

A lively salmon leaps into a turbulent water flow. *Scotland in Focus/David Hay.*

Sometimes there's a fish ladder to ease the trauma of the upstream passage, like the one at the hydro dam at Pitlochry which has become such a popular visitor attraction, but my favourite salmon leap is at the Falls of Rogie high above Strathpeffer where the hill water of the west rushes down to the lowland plain of Easter Ross. Mesmerised by sight and sound of unceasing water flow, the senses spring back into focus each time a big fish takes a dramatic leap.

Salmon have been synonymous with the Scottish scene for so long that they feature in the Glasgow coat of arms, while their Norse name 'lax' is incorporated into the names of western lochs and rivers like Laxford and Laxdale. The spears with which they were taken from bountiful river pools can be seen preserved in places like the Highland Folk Museum at Kingussie. But although I've heard time and again that Scottish servants actually stipulated to their masters that they shouldn't be served up salmon more than a certain number of times per week, it seems far harder to pin down actual records of such agreements.

Flowers of the field

FINE August days bring a frenzy of harvest activity to the farmlands. There was a time when folk spoke of cornfields; now country talk is as likely to be of cereal-producing units, and in the giant fields that stretch from the Laigh of Moray, through Strathmore to the arable lands of East Lothian and down to The Merse, it's as though the flowers of the old cornfields had never been at all. Yet their very names — corn marigold, cornflower and corn cockle — evoke a colourful countryside past, a vanished age when their mass flowering cheered the face of the land. Indeed, so great a show was there that one northern parish minister complained last century that the fields around his country kirk were more worthy of the attention of a botanist than of his farming parishioners.

But these are departed days, and with them has gone the lovely corn cockle, while the blue-flowered cornflower has almost followed

Nodding blue flowers of Scots bluebell brighten the passing summer days.
Scotland in Focus/Laurie Campbell.

the same path. Yet my faith in the capacity of Nature to bounce back in our country places is given a yearly boost by the sight of great golden drifts of corn marigolds springing up wherever the land is disturbed, confirming the viability of seeds that have been patiently biding their time deep down in the soil.

Seaside gems

SEASIDE plants have an attraction of their own. Though for many the freshness may now be fading, August shore days can be uplifting still in the beauty of their flowering. The Scots bluebell — harebell in the south — now comes into its own, nodding its delicate blue flower bells in the breeze. Sometimes nature seems to have missed out on the colouring, and pale, even white, bells provide a contrast to the delicate colouring of the typical flowers. Eyebright and yellow rattle open in the lee of the 'quiverin' girse' of the seaside bents, but the mauve field gentian with its pointed flower heads holds back a while yet, to brighten the salt-sprayed turf in later days.

The glaucous-leaved oyster plant, a sadly declining gem of northern sea shores. *Douglas Willis.*

The Scots lovage shares the bluebell's nationalist tag. By now its strong green herb leaves begin to lose their vigour, but not without a last, splendid end-of-season show of yellows and gold before decay comes and a return to the rock clefts and storm beach whence they came.

Happily, lovage and bluebell will long continue to brighten our summer shores. Sadly, the exquisite oyster plant may not. *Mertensia maritima* — even its scientific name provides alliterative pleasure — is declining throughout its British range which, in effect, is predominantly a Scottish one. My favourite oyster plant beach is by an eastern firth where the blue-green leaves and purplish-blue flowers trail over a background of pale seawashed sandstone boulders that highlight its charm. The fleshy leaves are said to taste of oysters, but I wouldn't know; it would seem such sacrilege to rob this hard-pressed gem of even one leaf.

The maddening midge

NOTHING is guaranteed to spoil a fine summer evening more than a plague of midges. But, as generations of visitors have discovered, the West Coast seems to have bred a super race with an appetite for tourist flesh. I never venture into the summer hills without a well-filled tube of the latest anti-midge cream, for this is one occasion when I'm all in favour of chemical warfare.

Not being a pipe smoker myself, I must confess to having a certain envy of those friends who envelop themselves in a blue cloud of tobacco smoke guaranteed even to deter the most determined of 'midgie' storm troopers. Mind you, it does have its disadvantages as an evening on a Highland marsh demonstrated all too vividly for a friend who was intent on spotting a grasshopper warbler that was lying infuriatingly low among the rushes. After a fruitless squelching traverse back and fore (during which the bird practised its angler's reel impression incessantly), we were about to give up when the little brown shape flew into the air. Startled by the suddenness of its appearance, my friend spluttered down his pipe, sending a fiery ember straight into his eye, momentarily blinding him and ensuring that the furtive impressionist vanished totally unseen!

Garden stars

MID-AUGUST in the garden is predictable in its birdlife pattern. Spotty young robins scuffle about under bushes, cocking their heads sideways and staring impassively with big round eyes while I set about the weeds. Every day brings further reddening of breast feathers that will come to be a symbol of their aggressive claim to a place in the garden. Willow warblers which have ignored our garden all year now haunt it for days on end, combing and re-combing every branch of the birches for lurking insect life, and sometimes bursting into a snatch of song that's a last echo of days when the trees bore a fresher look.

But our real star turns in this predictable pageant of fading summer are the juvenile blackbirds who make their annual discovery that the fruits of our garden fuchsia are exceedingly good to eat. *Fuchsia magellanica* is an excellent shrub for the wildlife garden, with its attractive purple and red flowers and juicy fruits. It's quite vigorous, with a fairly wide spread if left unpruned, though ours bears no grudge when I take the secateurs to its branches. Young blackies have a particular passion for its fruits, and as the month wears on, their antics outside the kitchen window become more engaging by the minute. As the first rays of the early sun glint on dew-drenched leaves, the brown-feathered young blackies manage to get themselves thoroughly drookit by hauling at the pulpy fruits, each hearty tug sending a shower of glistening droplets into the morning air.

SEPTEMBER

'In autumn when the woods are red
And skies are grey and clear . . .'

ROBERT LOUIS STEVENSON

*I*T was a Sassenach poet who gave the most masterly summation of autumn's character as 'Season of mists and mellow fruitfulness', and no less now, in our more northerly setting, do the unfolding days of September begin to reflect the description. Keats pictured the bird scene, too, evoking days when:

'The redbreast whistles from a garden-croft;
And gathering swallows twitter in the skies.'

It all points to the way in which September subtly merges fading summer with the sometimes misty, but often glorious, days of autumn's beginning. It's a time for watching the gathering swallows, for avoiding the unwelcome attentions of drowsy wasps, and for sensing summer's end in all the varied sounds and sights of the September countryside. It's that point in the year when nature's seasonal efforts find greatest expression in the wild harvest of our country places. At its best, early September may be a welcome extension of summer, fine days to hold off that inevitable feeling of the year's decline. And given some good days towards its close, we may appreciate the more the colourful climax of the autumn countryside.

The floodgates open

IN the bird world, I like the start of the month for the breath of the northlands which the newly arrived migrants bring, as the floodgates open on the great end-of-summer clearance of Arctic breeding grounds. Waders, which not long before had fed by the slanting rays of the Midnight Sun in limitless tundra wastes, now find themselves

119

The long-billed curlew probes the mysteries of the mudflats on its autumn migration. *Scotland in Focus/Laurie Campbell.*

seeking suitable stopping places in a busy land. These are the days to savour the great bird gatherings on the mudflats of the eastern firths and estuaries: locations like the Cromarty Firth between the Black Isle and Easter Ross; Findhorn Bay on the Moray coast; Aberdeenshire's Ythan estuary; the open mouths of Tay and Forth on either side of the peninsula of Fife, and of the more modest Eden in between; and the tidal flats of Aberlady in East Lothian.

In all of nature's spectacles, there are few to compare with September's wader gatherings, when tight packs of airborne knot and godwit twist and turn in split-second movements that would easily outclass a Red Arrows display. By now, most of the incoming migrants have lost the rich colouring of their breeding grounds, but a few still sport the russet plumage of the brief Arctic summer.

Amongst the most attractive of our wader migrants are the bar-tailed godwits, with long legs and long bills the better to stalk the mudflats and probe the rich mysteries of the ooze. The neat little knot are masters of aerial manoeuvre, the play of estuarine light catching on their silvery plumage at each turn, highlighting the togetherness

Autumn images reflected on a Wester Ross lochan. *Douglas Willis.*

of every split-second change. Not for them a flight commander's intercom instruction to bank this way or that, but rather some innate ability that enables the pack to act as one in a way that defies human understanding.

At the ebb, the waders abandon their high-water roosts to follow the advancing line of freshly-revealed mud, till the turn of the tide forces their retreat once more. It's this movement before the inflowing water that long ago earned the knot its name, recalling one Knut (better known as Canute), who tried to make the incoming tide obey him. Dunlin, redshank, oystercatcher and curlew swell the ranks of this September immigration, with a sprinkling of less common species such as the dainty-billed curlew sandpipers, scaly-plumaged ruffs, and elegant black-tailed godwits to keep east-coast birdwatchers happy.

Early birds

BUT it's not just in the estuaries and firths that the interest lies. In the month's early days, I scan the sandy shorelines for sanderlings, little waders that seem to be modelled more on clockwork mice than on birds, as they run along the water's edge. Turnstones are longer-stay residents. According to the old adage, it's the early bird that catches the worm, but in the turnstone's case it's the early bird that catches the eye, for the summer breeding plumage of the new arrivals is quite something to behold. The tortoiseshell, black and white colouring and eye-catching body pattern lend an attraction that is tantalisingly short-lived, for the finery quickly fades into the sombre plumage of the darker days. Yet, even in their workaday winter garb they hold an interest still, for scientists have suggested that each turnstone along a winter shore has a subtly different plumage pattern. To the human eye, each may look the same, but not to a turnstone. It's thought that recognition of individuals does away with the need for energy-consuming squabbles over who's who along the shore.

Turnstones engrossed in a food search are an absorbing sight, using their beaks to turn over every stone and seaweed frond in quest of the living protein that may lurk underneath. And they're certainly not averse to less conventional food items when the mood takes them, for I once watched a little group cheerfully consuming diced carrots beside the outfall of the soup-canning factory at Peterhead Bay.

Furry fliers

BATS have always had a bad press, which is a great shame, for they're interesting little creatures. Early autumn evenings round our house wouldn't be the same without the flittering presence of tiny pipistrelles, hawking back and fore among insects drawn by the street lights. You get a lot of pipistrelles to the pound, for each tiny furry flier weighs in at only half an ounce. Pipistrelles are creatures of the night, hanging in the darkness of hollow trees and lofts by day. What they lack in bulk they make up for in technology, for their echo-locating mechanism ensures their success as insect hunters, and it's well programmed to keeping them away from people's hair — one of the old wives' tales that has made generations of folk shun the close company of these much misunderstood creatures. Fortunately, bats will take to roosting in nestboxes, so that a well-furnished wildlife garden will be mindful of the provision of a home for a few bats in its complement of nest boxes, though these should never be treated with wood preservative, for its noxious fumes have been the certain end of many a bat colony during house-loft improvements.

Short-eared owl, the moth-like daytime hunter of northern moors.
Scotland in Focus/Ken Taylor.

The fact is that all creatures of the night tend to be viewed with a certain suspicion. Owls suffer the same fate, and older folk still express their misgivings at seeing an owl sitting in broad daylight. A widespread belief was that it presaged the death of someone close. In fact, short-eared owls are invariably seen by day, for these bright-eyed moorland nesters hunt their prey in broad daylight, unlike the familiar hooting tawny owls which shun the brightness.

Flaming geans and flighting geese

ADVANCING days of autumn are matched by declining night temperatures, and the chilling phrase 'ground frost' returns to the weather forecaster's vocabulary. The result can be a rapid trans-formation of the broad-leaved trees and larch into a seasonal glory. Stevenson isn't the only Scottish poet to have written of this alchemy of autumn.

> *'And the autumn leaves are turnin'*
> *And the flame o' the gean trees burnin'.*

So wrote Violet Jacob in her poem 'The Gean Trees', putting powerfully into words that fiery glow that seems to set the geans alight on late September hillsides after a night or two of frost.

Sometimes it's possible to see them by mid-month, but more commonly it's towards its close that the first geese cohorts come winging in from the north, hurrying V-shaped skeins etched for a moment on to a canvas of blue sky and scurrying white cloud.

The excitement of their calling filters to the ground below, blending a touch of winter to come with those last sounds of summer past, the excited twittering of swallows and martins on the wires as they prepare for their Africa-bound exodus.

'Gathering swallows . . .'

SOMEHOW, despite all the weeks of gathering and buzz of swallow and martin activity around the village, I'm never quite prepared for the suddenness of their leaving. One day they're still there; a couple of

Fleeing the northland winter, arriving skeins of pinkfeet geese etch the autumn skies. *Scotland in Focus/Eric Middleton.*

days later they've all gone, but I can't recall exactly when it was that they left. Their weeks of gathering haven't been in vain, however, for a lot of prospective properties will have been examined with a view to speedy acquisition for nests on their return.

Squirrel squatters

By definition, cities are people-dominated places where wildlife must fit in where it can. And yet, there are many urban places where 'greening' has been a long-established tradition. Such a place is Edinburgh with the green ribbon of Princes Street Gardens as a pleasant foil for the encircling townscape. And close to the Water of Leith, the Royal Botanic Garden provides a vibrant green contrast to the inert stonework of the inner city.

For a small boy, wide-eyed with interest at the castle with impressive Mons Meg and her other flanking canonry and the Scott Monument with its extravagant sandstone embellishments, a visit to the capital was an experience indeed. But somehow the lowly white-tailed

125

The red squirrel, lively resident of northern forests.
Scotland in Focus/Laurie Campbell.

waterhens jerking across the well-vegetated pond of the Botanic Garden were of just as much fascination, for they were used to folk and as a result far more confiding than the scuttling residents of the ditches I knew at home.

Squirrels also call this city place their home — the bushy-tailed grey creatures that the Forestry Commission would rather we call tree rats instead, for they're anathema to the forester. Unlike the red squirrel, its grey counterpart is something of an illegal alien, having first gained entry to the country in ill-conceived introductions around stately homes, and through escapes from zoological gardens (including Edinburgh) in the early part of the century. But now the squirrel squatters have outstayed their welcome and are regarded as pests in forest plantations because of the damage they cause to growing trees.

Throughout the south its colonising success has led the grey squirrel into any favourable woodland environment, and in recent years the tide of its colonisation has lapped the very edge of the Highlands. Thankfully, it's only the scampering forms of red squirrels

I see on walks among our nearby pine plantations, and long may it remain that way, for their presence is a permanent reminder of the perils of thoughtless introductions.

And their presence among such valuable plants as the Royal Botanic Garden can boast, is decidedly not welcome to the gardeners. Summer days have meant days of plenty, with peanuts galore from dozens of well-meaning visitors, but in salting down a store of nuts for a rainy day, the squirrels cause mayhem among the marigolds — or more likely among the rather more exotic plants which happen to be in the soil where they scrape.

I've seen heaps of autumn crocus bulbs scattered about the paths of the Garden when they should be safely tucked up in bed for their leafless flowering. Shooting to reduce numbers is never a popular business and always risks a wave of human protest in a city situation. Unfortunately, the simple fact is that the more the animals are fed, the more young they can support and the greater the threat becomes to the plants which, after all, are what most people come to the Garden to enjoy in the first place.

September on the hills

SEPTEMBER days are good days for the coast, but they're rewarding for the hills as well, and few walks are more pleasant at this time than that through the Pass of Ryvoan from Speyside into the Cairngorms. On a late September day when the bracken was mellowing into matching tints of yellow and orange, I took the walk from Glenmore Lodge through the scree-lined narrow defile that leads into the mountains. Along the path there was time to pause among the gnarled old pines that crowd round An Lochan Uaine, the little Green Lochan, a quiet water body never lacking the strange-coloured tint from which it takes its Gaelic name.

The blueness of sky on that early autumn morning served to emphasise the green of the water beneath, its surface gently ruffled now and then by a breeze that soughed among the scaly-barked old pines. Past the red-roofed bothy of Ryvoan, where shieling cattle once grazed the green sward, only an occcasional meadow pipit disturbed the silence, till the rock-strewn summit of Bynack More appeared, and the burping calls of ptarmigan carried above the gusting of the high-level wind. Nature plays a cruel trick on these mountain birds at this time, turning summer plumage into premature winter white. Against the sombre backcloth of brown moor, a dozen of these Arctic grouse made striking contrast as they flighted across a dark ravine. I sense a never-ending thrill in meeting with ptarmigan among the high tops, for it's a bird only of the loftiest places, its burping welcome the certain reward for the long upwards slog.

Once, the Cairngorms were Monadh Ruadh, the Red Hills, and on that clear September day the old name had an appropriateness that had less to do with the colour of the rock than with the play of early autumn light on the mountain face. But even fine September days can quickly change at this high level, and beneath the gravel-strewn plateau with Ben Avon's protruding rocky tors, swirling cloud had begun to fill the hollows.

Beside the rushing burn I paused for a while from my descent. Nature will reveal all manner of hidden things when you take the trouble to look, and had I not stopped I would surely have missed the planing eagle which materialised from the thickening mist and vanished as quickly again over a skyline fretted by the outlines of deer. My reward for placing my hand on the mossy bank as I sat down was to make close contact with the clammy skin of a frog who'd been resting there not expecting to be troubled at such a height. It would be hard to say who got the greater surprise, but this puddock with a head for heights was taking no more chances, and in one great loup he had disappeared into the heather, leaving me to my descent among the swirling smoor.

Close encounters of a furry kind . . .

SUCH encounters of an unexpected kind are the stuff of countryside experience. In a similar way, I won't easily forget a first meeting one September evening with some of the Highlands' least known creatures. As I arrived (by long-standing invitation) at the isolated Wester Ross cottage, the nearby sea loch reflected the last of the day's sunshine. Dark shadows were falling over the tangled backcloth of rhododendron, rock and bare pine roots that stretched behind the house. Over the years, the old folks had shared the solitude with a family of pine martens whose home the shadowy tangle was.

The old man led me in from the front door to the neat little sitting room, offering me a chair facing the open kitchen door. Inside, his wife was busying herself with some food: a few jam sandwiches and an egg, carefully positioned inside the open window. I was totally unprepared for the closeness of the encounter when it came. I could feel my body tingle as I found myself staring into the inquisitive whiskered face of an adult marten that had appeared on the side of the sink. In a moment this beautiful beast with dark legs and tail and creamy-coloured bib had entered the room, taken a sandwich in its mouth, and disappeared. As it went, another took its place, lifted the egg and likewise vanished into the night. On an earlier evening, I was told that one of the martens had boldly walked into the sitting room while the bodach was taking his ease with his newspaper, had a sniff around and just as boldly walked out again!

After the joy of sharing the delight of the old folks in this meeting with their adopted wild family, I can thoroughly recommend pine marten watching as one of the most entrancing of wildlife contacts. Visitors parking their cars in the gloaming at some of the popular picnic areas in the North-west Highlands, where there are trees and rocks nearby, are sometimes rewarded these days by the sight of a furry raider at a litter bin, for some martens are as much into convenience foods as the black-headed gulls which haunt the same lay-bys by day.

Food for free

IN nature's wild harvest, berries play a key role in the support system of the countryside's birds and mammals at this time. As the month wears by, the starlings which have re-formed into flocks descend on the elder bushes and greedily relieve them of their black clusters. Rowans are meted out the same short, sharp treatment, as the starlings gorge themselves on berry after berry. Shiny red rose-hips are also tackled, even if it means a few attempts at forcing the hard fruits down their gullets.

The starling really is a much-maligned bird, suffering the censures of city authorities and pedestrians alike for the rain of droppings that descends on pavements on winter nights. It's no consolation, I suppose, that the seedling rowans and elders which sprout out of high-level lums and ledges are a free gift from the starling lodgers, each derived from a seed conveniently encased in its own starter-pack of fertiliser.

The truth is that the starling isn't just the dark-looking bird of familiar winter silhouette, but rather a striking combination of green and purple iridescence, enlivened by smart white spots. Fine September days are good times to appreciate it, when the sun's rays still shine strongly enough on the birds to highlight the finery of their plumage.

It's a rich bounty, the berry crop, acting as a magnet to the starlings, but they and the other harvesters of the seasonal riches don't have it all to themselves. Shiny black brambles make a rare feast, and whenever the end-of-month weather allows, we like to make a start to laying in our own family store of succulent berries to remind us in the dark days of the countryside in brighter times. Our particular favourite is a bramble mousse — a taste of the countryside's goodness to brighten the most depressing days that winter can bring.

In the absence of good brambling places nearby, it's an idea to plant one of the modern well-berried thornless brambles. Elders are really for the bigger garden where space isn't a concern . . . or where the urge to make elderflower wine is especially strong! But rowans are different, for a rowan near the front gate is a necessity if you feel that neighbourhood witches may be as troublesome as prowling felines! There's no end of variety to choose from, from the bright red native to the pale yellow berried 'Joseph Rock'. Not all rowan berries are equally appealing to the birds — which is fine if you want a colourful show, but not so good if you feel that yours is a true wildlife garden.

In the days before television viewing absorbed so much of children's leisure time, the countryside's autumn bounty was as much for them as for the birds. Firing rowan berries out of peashooters was once as popular a pastime among loons as cracking conkers on the end of a string. The Wars of the Roses can have been no more fiercely contested than our wars of the roddens, the pavements to and from the school being littered for days with ammunition well squashed under tackety boots.

Clearly, the rowan can be a tree for all purposes, but in seasonal terms it's above all the tree of early autumn, and I'd never be without at least one in the garden — even if the birds decide that their needs are greater than mine, and decline to leave me any berries to contemplate in September's fleeting days.

OCTOBER

*P*ERHAPS above all others, October is a month for all senses. As chill night air settles heavily over the land, the broad-leaved woodlands slip into a seasonal blend of colours that delights the eye by day, while bird migrants impress their calling upon the ear as they pass unseen by night. The smell of burning leaves mingling with the mist of evening lingers with a hint of sweetness in the heavy air, and there's a certain sensuous sensation in scuffling through the litter of fallen leaves on a woodland floor.

Redwings' return

FROM the moors of Galloway to the middle of Glasgow, above the hills of Donside and over the heart of Dundee, there's one October bird sound above all others to set the seal upon the season. It's that thin *tseep* call of the night; a seeming insignificance against the starry vastness above, or of the roar of city traffic below, but one which tells of the redwings' return from the northlands. As the month wears through, these smart migrants with the give-away russety-red oxters forsake their Scandinavian breeding grounds and pour into Scotland in their thousands. Their calling is their contact in the unending blackness of the night sky, instinctively charting their course by the pattern of the stars.

Daylight sees the new thrush arrivals hungrily devouring the berry crop along roadside hedges. Fieldfares — larger and greyer, with pale napes that resemble judges' wigs — swell the redwing ranks in a food-for-free bonanza, their harsher *tchak, tchak, tchak* calls a sure

Redwing: the unseen migrant of dark autumn nights.
Scotland in Focus/Laurie Campbell.

guide to their presence. Sometimes the communal feasting attracts a mistle thrush or two — impressively large and heavily spotted birds with a churring call that is unmistakeable in its volume and carrying power.

It's strange how out-of-place the last birds of summer can seem on an October day. Swallows and house martins, which only a week or two before were so familiar a part of the scene, seem forlornly misplaced now in a countryside rapidly filling with winter visitors. Yet, a few late-fledged birds often remain about, long after the main contingent has departed for the warmer south.

Twitchers' delight

THINGS don't always go smoothly for some of the autumn bird travellers, as 'twitchers', that band of ultra-enthusiastic, go-anywhere at anytime bird spotters, know well. Migrants setting out from northern Europe in clear weather conditions may find themselves disorientated when the sky becomes obscured, and given a south-east wind to drift them towards our shores, North Sea oil platforms have more than helicopters flying in, while all sorts of unusual visitors make landfall along the eastern seaboard. It's a time for birdwatchers to expect the unexpected. Wrynecks and bluethroats, black redstarts and barred warblers, and a list of rarities besides, are manna from heaven for birdwatchers at island outposts such as Fair Isle, North Ronaldsay, and the Isle of May off the Fife coast, where bird observatories monitor the seasonal passage.

When the wind blows resolutely from the west, there's little cheer to be seen among the birdwatchers at a bird observatory. Professor M. F. M. Meiklejohn often stayed on the Isle of May at migration time, amusing fellow birdwatchers with his poetic additions to the observatory log. During one such unrewarding spell, the Professor felt moved to append the following little ditty:

> 'There was an old man on the May
> Who knelt on the North Ness to pray:
> 'Oh, Lord, I have sinned —
> But why need the wind
> Blow westerly day after day?''

It was the same learned birdwatcher who suggested that the small brown birds which nobody can ever identify, plus the sundry other things that disappear before being properly noted, should be classed under the name of 'hoodwink'. Unfortunately, I must confess to having met with a positive host of autumn hoodwinks in my time.

But you don't have to be on an island to share in the migrant mania. Headlands make good watching spots, too, and bird 'falls' lend autumn interest to such places as Rattray Head in Aberdeenshire, Tentsmuir Point and Fife Ness on the Fife peninsula, and St Abb's Head in Berwickshire. I recall the excitement of a rare bluethroat among the Brussels sprouts at a Girdleness allotment at Aberdeen, and the disbelief in seeing an even rarer red-breasted flycatcher snatching insects among our dahlias one misty morning in the red granite heart of Peterhead. The irony was that the stranger was soon chased off by our resident garden robin, a bird either myopic or determined that anything with a red-breast should be seen off the premises, no matter how rare. But retribution was just around the corner, for within hours a passing kestrel had pounced on the robin and carried it away.

Sometimes more familiar species are involved in the mass October arrivals, blackbirds and robins in particular making landfall in the east in their thousands. Even goldcrests, so tiny for undertaking such hazardous journeys, may turn up on foggy mornings in surprising abundance, and at such times their thin calling echoes among settings as unlikely as marram-covered sand dunes and black-tarred salmon fishers' bothies.

Wildfowl and wild places

OF all Scotland's wildlife experiences, the one that stirs me most is the mass arrival of the goose flocks at the lochs and marshes of their traditional gathering grounds. The open waters around St Serf's Island and the nearby ruined walls of the old castle of Loch Leven in Fife ring to the mass arrival of pinkfooted geese, skein after excited skein pitching down on the water after their long flight from the volcanic wastelands of Iceland.

In that desolate island fortress the unfortunate Mary Queen of Scots was imprisoned in less settled times. I've a special liking for such places with a strong mix of wildlife and historical interest, for the one seems to complement the other, a sense of the past lending atmosphere to places that resound to nature's wild chorus. At the RSPB's Vane Farm educational centre on the south side of the loch, it's possible to see not only the multitude of geese but the concentrations of duck such as mallard, teal, wigeon and shoveler for which the loch is internationally important, and to learn much about the place itself.

Valley wetlands

TAKEN overall, there's really very little of Scotland's countryside that hasn't been taken in hand and 'improved' in some way or another, and not always to the advantage of wildlife. The tide of agricultural improvement last century removed much of the wetland interest, especially along the more fertile river valleys. But sometimes nature was less submissive, and the valley wetlands that resisted the onslaught have taken on new value in terms of their wildlife interest.

The sinuous beauty of whooper swans is reflected on many Scottish winter lochs. *Scotland in Focus/Laurie Campbell.*

Nowhere is this more evident that at the Insh Marshes, that vast tract of marsh, sedge and willow scrub in the shadow of the Cairngorms in Strathspey. I like the railway journey to and from the Highland capital at this time — and right throughout the winter, for that matter — for the fact that the line skirts the edge of the flooded marshland where whooper swans have gathered from time immemorial. At the passage of a train across the embankment, the swans lift their necks stiffly, trails of dripping weed dangling from yellow-marked black bills.

On a sunny morning towards the end of the month there are few sights to compare with that of the whoopers mirrored white on the water against a backcloth of high hills touched by the fresh snows of winter. The scene recalls W. B. Yeats's poem with ethereal strands woven into verses where the wild swans

> '*drift on the still water,*
> *Mysterious, beautiful.*'

But the Insh Marshes are not the only valley place where nature has refused to be subdued. In the south-west, the high water-table in the Dee's flood plain creates an attraction for large gatherings of geese. In that corner of the country, greylags are rather upstaged by Greenland white-fronts, rarer birds by far, for their breeding grounds are restricted to the desolation of the Arctic island from which they take their name. The wildlife interest of the area has been recognised in the designation of the Ken-Dee marshes as an RSPB nature reserve, another splendid place at which to see not only the geese, but whooper swans and several duck species as well, with a chance of spotting one of the hen harriers which haunt the winter marshes.

Given a fine October day when geese formations wing noisily in to marsh or loch, it's impossible to be unmoved by the sheer wild exuberance of the scene. In European terms, it can easily be said that in our wildfowl wintering places, Scotland can claim some of the best remaining wildlife spectacles in the whole of the continent.

'*All the birds of the world . . .*'

IN our age, it's easy to turn to a bird book or watch a television programme that will extend our wildlife knowledge. How different for the Scottish naturalists of old, working without bird books or binoculars, yet building up their own picture of their wildlife heritage.

Thomas Edward was a nineteenth-century pioneer, whose thirst for natural history drew him away from his shoemaker's awl and last in Banff to tramp the North-east coast. Although we're decades apart in time, Edward's path seems often to have crossed with mine. As a Buchan loon smitten by the birdwatching bug, I spent many a rainy day in Peterhead's Arbuthnot Museum, avidly studying the cases of stuffed birds. Many of the faded specimens had been collected and mounted by Edward himself.

The Banff souter and I shared a passion for Buchan's best wildlife place of all — the Loch of Strathbeg that lies beyond Mormond Hill, just along the coast from the fishing port of Fraserburgh. Here Edwards was mesmerised by the spectacle for which Strathbeg is still noted on October days — the mass arrival of its wildfowl, for this curving sheet of water is a strategic stopping-place on the great flight paths along which wildfowl converge on Scotland from north and east.

Like Loch Leven, the Loch of Strathbeg is worth a visit at this time, for this shallow coastal lagoon is a place where past and present are interwoven in a setting of rich atmosphere. By the shores of the loch stand the ruins of St Mary's Chapel, last reminder of the lost village of Rattray, a community doomed to die when its harbour

The Loch of Strathbeg — Buchan's wildfowl mecca. *Douglas Willis*.

mouth was sealed by sand in the great storm which cut off the loch. But the people's loss was to be nature's gain, for the freshwater loch became a major wildlife refuge. 'All the birds of the world come here in winter' was Thomas Edward's reaction to Strathbeg's wildfowl riches, and it's no less impressive today with its vast gatherings of pinkfeet and greylag geese, whooper swans and assorted duck species. To stand by the loch as the wind whistles among the crumbling walls of that last reminder of the lost village (the air is never still in Buchan!) as the yelping skeins come whiffling in against fiery sunset skies, is to share in a countryside experience of rare quality.

It was at the Loch of Strathbeg that, as a boy, I set eyes on so many wildfowl species for the first time. Mingled with the familiar there was often the unfamiliar, too, like the sight once of a trio of snow geese banking against towering North Sea clouds, their black wing tips standing out in sharp contrast to the brilliant white backcloth behind; or the spectacle of hundreds of whoopers on the surface of the loch, like the aftermath of some unseasonable blizzard; and the moment I saw a mute swan panicked into clattering take-off by the unexpected surfacing of an otter beneath it.

For some reason, Strathbeg attracts the exotic, too, like a flamingo which used to flight out to feed with the whooper swans. The first time I saw the bizarre sight of the long-shanked pink bird with the pure white whoopers in a field some miles from the loch, I was so excited that I raced up to the nearby farmhouse to tell the farmer. However, I was put firmly in my place when he looked at me and said, 'O aye, it's been aboot wi' the swans a year or twa noo.'

In the frenzy of North Sea oil and gas activity that gripped North-east Scotland in the early seventies, it was proposed to pass a pipeline through the dunes and loch and to develop a gas processing plant by its side. For employment-starved Buchan, 'Jobs versus ducks' was perhaps a predictable media headline, but in a newspaper article which I wrote, I suggested that the loch deserved better, for it had such educational potential for the future. Immediately afterwards I was attacked in the same newspaper columns for entertaining such a daft notion. In the end, however, the gas plant was established along the coast at St Fergus, the sand dunes were unbreached, and the loch was left to its birds. Now its wildfowl riches remain as a local, national, and even international asset. And thanks to the RSPB's enthusiastic first warden, Jim Dunbar, the nature reserve has indeed taken on that important educational rôle for local children.

Patterns of the hairst

VIOLET Jacob's lines are an evocation of October days throughout the length of the eastern lowlands where geese flight above fields marked by giant straw bales and the raked lines of barley stubbles that follow the harvest. Once, the patterns of the hairst were etched on Scotland's farmlands in very different ways. The days of combine and stook have now long faded from the big arable farms of the east, but they linger on in the north where fields are small, and crofters supply the hand labour needed to maintain the old traditions.

Travelling along the coastal fringe of East Sutherland and Caithness on an October day last year, I chanced upon a pleasing reminder of hairst days of long ago in the ranks of drying corn stooks. In one dyke-enclosed clifftop field, around fifty slate-grey rock doves had descended upon the stooks, greedily cramming their crops as if expecting to be chased away at any time. For the sake of the corn, I hope that they were, for it would have been a pity for the crofter to have been poorly rewarded for his labours in providing such a pleasing autumn picture, and a reminder of how things used to be.

Harvest scene, Strathmore, in the early 1970s — a last reminder of the days of combine and stook. *Douglas Willis*.

Fly agaric, the fairytale fungus of autumn days. *Douglas Willis*.

Fungal forays

IN the year's progress, it's obvious that the fresh growth of spring must have an antithesis in the fading decline of autumn, and out of the dying season's growth comes forth an annual crop of fungi to feast on the decay. Our local golf course is combed for brown-gilled mushrooms at this time, and advertisements appear in the local newspapers wanting chanterelles to tickle some foreign palate, but my own fungal forays are as much to admire the often forgotten beauty of these strange denizens of the autumn woods. For sheer flamboyance, though, there's nothing to match the fly agaric, that white-spotted red toadstool of birch and pine woods so beloved of children's book illustrators. Nature's adhesive doesn't seem to be quite what it might be in the case of the fly agaric, for the white spots have a habit of dropping off as the toadstool opens out. In this regard, they've a certain passing resemblance to those bakers' creations known as 'sair heidies' in the North-east, consisting of a sponge cake with a paper 'bandage' round the side, for the pieces of sugar on the top invariably drop off as you try to eat them.

Mention of book illustrators and toadstools is a reminder that

140

there was more to Beatrix Potter than Peter Rabbit and Mrs Tiggy-Winkle (a character based on an old Highland washerwoman whom she knew in Perthshire). In a recent exhibition of the artist's work, I was pleasantly surprised to find that she had also produced some outstanding fungal studies.

Compared to birds and flowers, mushrooms and toadstools seldom exercise the brush of countryside artists, but not so with Beatrix Potter who had a rare talent for portraying them in all their complex and sometimes bizarre form and symmetry. The woods around Birnam and Dunkeld where the family stayed during the salmon-fishing season on the Tay furnished her with ample subject matter. She was also fortunate in having the help of her friend Charlie Macintosh, Perthshire naturalist and local postie, who supplied her with parcels of fresh specimens when she was at home in the south. Perth Museum and Art Gallery is fortunate to have some fine examples of Beatrix Potter's fungal portraiture not far from the woods from which the living subjects sprung.

Echoes of the past

ON fine October days when the harvest is in and the cries of wild geese fill the air, a new sound drifts across our Black Isle farmlands. It's the excited baaing of blackfaced sheep newly decanted out of floats which have transported them from the west — sometimes from as far away as Skye — where grazing is scarce to spend the winter days among the stubble and neep parks of the eastern fringe. It's a sight and sound I greatly enjoy, for in the noisy confusion of the new arrivals is a last echo of the old transhumance which was part of the way of life of upland farmers everywhere. The shielings of Scotland had their last active use on the open moors of Lewis, but in earlier times they had a parallel in the saeters of Norway and the alps of Switzerland — a people's response to an environment unable to supply all the livestock's feeding in the one place.

Our Black Isle blackfaces are at first unwilling guests, pining for the unrestrained freedom of their western moors, unwilling to be confined within the square outlines of a farm park. These early days can be a sore trial to the farmers, too, making all too clear the inadequacies of their fencing, as wily sheep shamelessly exploit the smallest gap and set merrily off on their travels.

Scottish blackface on a grey drystane dyke. *Scotland in Focus/Gordon Stevenson.*

Hill sheep are part of the very fabric of Scottish farming life, for they've helped shape the face of our upland landscape. The great sheep hirsels which crop the Border hills are a reminder of ancient days when wealth was counted in fleece, and great abbey buildings could be raised on the strength of it. In material terms, too, the sheep have left their stamp on the land in the never-ending drystane dykes which line the hill faces and in the great circular fanks or stells, things of mellowness and beauty in themselves and a tribute to the drystane dykers who circumscribed them in stone gathered from the land. And where other places might have a statue of some famous figure, the Borders town of Moffat appropriately has a curly-horned ram overseeing its ongoings.

Who knows what the Borders sheep think of the haughty-looking llamas now being reared above St Mary's Loch in Ettrick Forest for their fine hair fibres? On narrow Highland roads I much prefer to meet a characterful blackface than to chance upon a peelie-wally Cheviot, for the latter seem stupid, unpredictable beasts, liable to bound in front of the bonnet at any moment for no reason whatsoever.

The blackface road users, by contrast, usually obey the Green Cross Code, waiting for a car to pass by or leaving a good safety margin as they cross in front, with a wag of stumpy tails by way of cheery greeting.

Autumn in Assynt

RICH though the east may be in its wildlife interest, I always find a crossing to the west a worthwhile effort, for an October journey has its own rewards, especially when autumn allows the countryside to show her best face. In one such magic spell, I found Stac Pollaidh obliging with a warmth and clarity to rival summer days and make its craggy summit ridge fairly shimmer. As I climbed the mountain's steep upper face, a black raven sallied forth from the crags, croaking his indignation as he sailed away into the distance. Yellowing birch trees margined the long shores of Loch Lurgainn below, while from Loch an Doire Dhuibh behind the mountain itself, and over towards the outlined massif of Cul Mor, came the echoing roar of stags, hurling their defiance across the loneliness of peat flow and dubh lochan. In earlier days these lonely expanses echoed to the plaintive calling of greenshank, the bird of the Highland peat flows, but now the place had fallen silent, save for the roaring of the deer.

Peat seems to be a much neglected aspect of the Scottish scene. So many of the lowland peat mosses, such as the vast carse lands of the Forth, have been tamed, but in the north peat is the ever-present blanket over the ancient bare rock below. Formed from plants that hold the water like a sponge and modify the processes of decomposition, the peat bogs are interesting tapestries of subdued colouring. Older folk recall the tragic days when so many men left the straths and coastlands of the Highlands to engage in the gory warfare of the trenches, and how, as children, they gathered and squeezed dry the sphagnum moss that it might be used to staunch the bloody flow of shattered veins in hurried field dressings.

In that same glorious spell of October weather, I stopped for a while in Assynt, a little further to the north, whose expanses of sullen peat bog are dramatically broken by towering Quinag and Canisp, and the rearing sugar loaf peak of Suilven. These survivors from an ancient past had assumed an unreal look, the effect heightened by the blue mist of morning clinging to the ground and making the mountain tops rear dramatically upwards, as if floating free of any base. Recently-arrived redwings exploded out of roadside rowans heavy still with autumn's unconsumed fruit. Beyond the waterside birches, a pair of dippers followed the blueness of the river flow, while a far-off buzzard wheeled and mewed across the stillness. A stoat darted about his furtive business among tussocks of lifeless deer grass sapped by the advance of a season now drawing the salmon upstream to seek their spawning places and to ripple the slack of backwater pools. On one distant peak it seemed that winter had already come, but the sparkling whiteness was only the glint of sunshine on summit rock screes, shattered reminders of ancient times when a band of sparkling quartzite once rested above the Torridonian Sandstone beds.

Assynt is an ancient land, its face infinitely slowly fashioned through the aeons of time. In human terms it's a lonely, at times unwelcoming, place where nature sets strict limits on man's endeavour. But autumn had brought its own loveliness that day, cheering the land with the reddened brightness of rowan leaves and the blueness of the water's flow. All too soon the berries would be stripped and the thrushes on their way, October's fleeting colours would drain from the face of the land, and the hoodie crows would retreat sullenly into their moorland backcloth once more. But for the moment, in the warmth and colour of that Indian Summer day, even the hoodies had lost their inhibitions and were unashamedly sun-worshipping on the river bank, grateful for the rare gift of such a glorious Highland day.

NOVEMBER

'... The fowls of heaven,
Tamed by the cruel season, crowd around
The winnowing store ...'

JAMES THOMSON

*T*HERE'S something special about a winter wood. To walk among the trees is an experience at once calming and disturbing in its total peacefulness, for there's a multitude of places where the low rays of winter sun never penetrate, mossy green corners that exude their dankness into the heavy air of morning.

Yet, all is far from unrelieved gloom and decay at this early winter time. The scuffling of a blackbird in the leaf litter along a woodland edge, the clatter of a wood pigeon roused from its peaceful roosting place high among the branches, the melancholic song of a robin from the dark depths of a plantation — these are the sounds of November woodland days.

'Down in the forest ...'

FOREST walks, whether along officially recognised routes or less formally by way of roads and tracks, tend to be thought of as summer pursuits, but winter walking among the trees brings its own rewards. With luck, the ringing of a crossbill may echo through the stillness of a conifer planting, but as often as not, this bird appears only in lofty silhouette, its curiously crossed mandibles making short work of the toughest pine cones, before dropping the opened remains to the ground below.

Blue tit and coal tit forget for now their family differences and unite in flittering flocks that criss-cross the woods. Sometimes a few goldcrests join the party, calling thinly all the while as they investigate the mysteries of the insect life concealed among the upper branches.

145

Tits are inquisitive little birds which can be persuaded to come in about by any unusual sound, such as the penetrating squeaky noise made by sucking the back of the hand. I'm not quite sure what they think it is, but it certainly can draw an interested audience.

In northern plantations, there's sometimes an insistent churring among the tit flocks. *Parus cristatus scoticus*, the Scottish crested tit, is more easily identified by its calling and crest than by its body colouring, for it sports an unremarkable hodden grey sort of plumage pattern. Finding no attraction in more southerly forests, it remains faithful to its northern heartland among the old Caledonian pines. However, this distinctive emblem of the Scottish Ornithologists' Club has now expanded out of Speyside into forestry plantings in the surrounding areas, and our local Black Isle birds have found a niche in the old Scots pine stands dating from the earlier days of the Forestry Commission. When a particularly inquisitive crested tit comes close by, I half expect it to land on my hand, as they do along well-frequented forest paths in the Grisons in Switzerland, lured in by visitors' offerings of peanuts. The trouble is that the local red squirrels are drawn to the same hand-outs, and my memories of handfeeding crested tits in the Alps are tinged by recollections of an unnerving moment when, out of the blue, a bushy-tailed squirrel shot up the outside of my trouser leg, sharp little claws painfully marking its progress as it ascended at high speed to snatch a nut from my fingers.

Sometimes the calls of redpolls and siskins mingle among the tree tops, as mixed flocks travel through a plantation. Both are tiny birds, easily missed but well worth looking for. Redpolls take their name from a rosy blaze on the forehead of the dapper little cock birds. The neat cock siskin is no less perky as he hangs from conifer branches, his yellow-green body feathering and smart black cap setting him apart from the other finches.

Though essentially a forest bird, the siskin often forsakes its natural home these days to try its luck among town and suburban gardens, its presence being one of the success stories of the bird feeding movement. The ubiquitous plastic bags of peanuts appear to have done the trick, drawing them like magnets. The siskin's normal feeding methods of clinging sideways and upside down to conifer

Blue tit: lively garden resident. *Scotland in Focus/Roger Fox.*

branches are ideal for hanging on to the net bags. In fact, in our village, where the red bags brighten many a winter bush, there are weeks on end when the sound of siskin to-ing and fro-ing is never out of the air. But they're an enigma, too, disappearing for days on end, then making a sudden and welcome reappearance.

Highland feline

THE familiar artist's image of snarling, sabre-fanged wildcat is hardly the memory I retain from my occasional meetings with these elusive beasts. Each encounter invariably follows the same pattern: a brief sighting, followed by a rapid disappearance, for they're creatures which shun the company of man — and with good reason, too, for far too often they're shot without justification. A full-grown wildcat is an impressive sight. Fleet of foot and rangy-looking, a wildcat ran for yards in front of my car one November night, racing through the swirl of snowflakes in the wild freedom so often denied its kind, for

The tabby-patterned wildcat is a well-camouflaged resident of rough terrain. *Scotland in Focus/Ray Chaplin.*

they're snared, trapped, mutilated and shot in a latter-day flowering of that Victorian prejudice which robbed our countryside of sea eagle, osprey and kite and threatened the pine marten, too.

Many ordinary cats have taken to the wild, but they're never true wildcats, animals well-built of body and well-endowed of tail — a broad-ended, black-hooped brush of a thing, unlike the tapering termination of a domestic cat gone wild. The tabby markings serve them well in their need to blend with the wild country they inhabit. From time to time I see one that has fallen foul of gun or car, and even in death the creature impresses.

Occasionally there are reports of big felines, sometimes black in colour, roaming the northern countryside. The Kellas Cat of Morayshire recently attained rapid fame in this way, for there's always a fascination with big cats, and the longer they are of tooth, the more the fascination. Some large beasts are thought to be the progeny of a wildcat tom which has mated with a domestic animal.

Such is public interest in any suggestion of a big cat on the loose, that the reported sighting of a puma in Inverness-shire some years ago was guaranteed to hit the national headlines. But Felicity the puma, who was eventually cornered and caught, was thought to be an animal unused to the ways of the wild. She passed her last days at the Highland Wildlife Park at Kincraig near Kingussie. And now, even in death, she continues to have a steady stream of admirers, for she reposes within a glass case in Inverness Museum.

Though currently not sporting any more escaped pumas, the Highland Wildlife Park is a fascinating place to visit, with its representative collection of Highland wildlife, past and present, and an opportunity to glimpse a wildcat in comparative close-up.

High above Loch Insh with its bright blue surface and dark fringing pines, a bloodcurdling howl carries across the hillside. Wolves! Though exterminated from their last Scottish refuge but a few miles away in the eighteenth century, these much-maligned creatures still make their presence felt in the Strathspey countryside. But now they're safely (for their sake, not ours) behind wire, and are a major attraction at Kincraig.

Above the Insh Marshes with their featureless acres of reed, European bison now share the slopes with mouflon, red deer and pale-muzzled wild horses. Massive brown bears cavort and splash in the pool inside their enclosure and Arctic foxes reflect the changing seasons in their turn of coat.

149

Most of all, I enjoy an occasional visit to Kincraig for the opportunity to come close to badger and otter at home, as it were, for both have been provided with indoor sleeping quarters visible to visitors through sheets of plate glass. In their bracken-filled set, the nocturnal badgers twitch and snore the day away, oblivious to the comings and goings behind the glass, while sleek-coated otters lie curled as they would lie up unseen in their holts in the wild.

Winter feeding

NOVEMBER is the best month to start winter feeding the garden birds, for it's a time when natural food supplies are diminishing, and few things give more pleasure than a lively gathering of birds at a garden feeding station. A 'station' may sound like a rather grand affair, but it's really just a particular place, preferably outside a window, where birds are regularly fed. Many households are content to throw out a few scraps of bread for the birds, but bread on its own doesn't supply the kind of diet needed to maintain good condition when the hard weather comes.

Bird cakes are a good idea, and many and varied are the recipes for them, but they're usually variations on a fat and seed theme, with melted fat poured into some kind of container and allowed to solidify along with the added seeds and nuts before hanging it up for the birds to peck at. Home-made efforts, like a filled half-coconut, are cheaper, of course, but if the budget can stretch to a regular supply of commercially-produced feeding items, there's no lack of choice these days. Winter Larder, manufactured at Alness, is an enterprising fat and seed product now marketed in stores and garden centres throughout the country, and the firm responsible is almost 'By Appointment' to the birds, being the official supplier of the RSPB's centenary bird cake!

Setting the table

REGULAR feeding not only affords pleasure in bird watching, but can be a positive effort for conservation as well. Many birds survive a cold winter because of the regular supply of food, but feeding, once

Though forest birds by origin, siskins now find winter nut bags an irresistible attraction. *Scotland in Focus/Ken Taylor.*

started, should continue on a regular basis, for they will come to depend on it, and in severe weather hungry birds may waste valuable food-searching time in hanging around waiting for food that never comes.

A bird-table is the best way of providing food, and should be made cat-proof, by placing it at a resonable height above the ground. An open wooden tray, with a lip round the edge to stop the food being blown away, has the advantage of providing clear all-round views of the bird visitors, but has the drawback of allowing the food to become waterlogged during wet weather. A covered table is probably best, and commercially-produced versions are easily obtained at garden centres or from specialist manufacturers. These vary from the useless (the type that's little more than a wee house on top of a stick) to the highly successful ones which allow plenty of access for the birds, like that in the RSPB catalogue.

Some birds aren't keen to feed on a raised table. Dunnocks, sometimes known as hedge sparrows, are real 'snappers-up of unconsidered trifles', and prefer to mouse around on the ground beneath. Their needs can be catered for by sprinkling some food under the bird-table or beneath nearby bushes.

Birds need plenty of water, even in the coldest days of winter, so a feeding station should include some sort of drinking receptacle. In times of hard frost, water containers freeze over, but the birds still depend on a constant supply. Surprisingly, they'll also bathe in the worst excesses of winter weather, for they must keep their plumage in good order. In fact, it's no unusual thing to see starlings and blackies having a good dook in freezing roadside puddles.

The great thing about a bird-table is that you just never know who's going to visit it. Among our most unexpected visitors have been a beautiful male brambling and a sparrowhawk, though, to be honest, the latter was more interested in eating the other diners than in consuming the food on the table. I feel envious of those fowk who enjoy the regular sight of great-spotted woodpeckers at their bird tables, and it's in the same sort of woodland fringe gardens that squirrels — alien grey and native red — sometimes share the birds' supply of nuts, though the prize for the most unexpected visitor should probably go to the pine martens which frequent some Highland bird-tables.

In gardens visited by cats, it's important to safeguard the birds from unwelcome attentions, which is why a raised table is best. Given a safe feeding place, the same birds will come back day after day. Some become fiercely territorial as they feed, siskin cocks, for example, spending much of their time threatening and persuading one another to push off and find their own nut bag.

Pine martens are well-practised hunters, little troubled by snowy days. *Scotland in Focus/Ray Chaplin.*

152

Lichens can grow on you!

ON winter days, when the colour has largely drained from the face of the land, the lichens which grow from rocks and trees assume a fresh interest. Some are yellow and bright on seaside rocks where summer gulls have splashed them with guano. Others are grey and dull, like the straggly growth festooning the branches of a winter wood. On West Coast rocks, absorbing abstract pictures are painted by lichen growth on faces smoothed by the passage of time. Perhaps one of the best known of the old country dyes was crotal, a crusty lichen of the rocks which gives a reddish-brown colour with a long history of use in Harris tweed.

Seals and selkies

THE eastern firths of Scotland are havens for the common seal. Appropriately, its other name is firth seal, and in open estuaries like the Tay and inside the Cromarty and Beauly Firths they can be seen lying on the mudflats when the tide is low, bodies curved in the shape of an old-fashioned baby's feeding bottle as the wind dries their sleek fur coats.

The grey seal is an altogether larger animal, and in world terms decidedly uncommon. Yet, whenever conditions are to its liking it occurs in great colonies around our western shores, the white-coated pups being born on land in the autumn months. From North Rona round to North Ronaldsay, the island waters of the west resound to the crooning of the seals. An islet called the Barrel of Butter in Scapa Flow gets its name from the rent once paid for the privilege of taking seals there. In the North Isles of Orkney, folk once made slippers called rivlins out of sealskin, and many were the strange tales of selkie folk recounted by the winter firesides in island crofts. The inquisitive seals have much to answer for in coastal folklore, the caves around Cromarty long having a reputation as a haunt of mermaids. Grey seals are nothing if not adventurous, moving right up river systems at

In the dark days of winter, lichens conjure up memories of bright summer scenes. Sandaig. *Douglas Willis.*

times of high water to prey on unsuspecting fish in freshwater bodies. On one occasion, the Nature Conservancy Council warden at Loch Maree informed me that there were no fewer than eight of these great beasts in the loch at one time.

Looking ahead

THERE may still be time to put up a nest box somewhere around the garden, allowing time for any preservative to weather, and for birds to become accustomed to its presence. Many garden centres supply nest boxes these days, but they sometimes go for the aesthetic rather than the practical. It's not necessary to have a rustic finish, and besides, the bark often falls away in time, giving an unattractive appearance. Nor are birds struck on the idea of having a convenient little perch stuck outside the entrance hole, for they much prefer to fly in directly. A useful type of box is the two-in-one model which, with the front section and small round entrance hole in position, will attract tits, or which, with this detachable section removed, may provide a desirable residence for birds such as robins. Even owls can be attracted by the right type of box. A wide variety of nest boxes can be obtained from such experienced suppliers as the RSPB, Jamie Wood, and the Scottish National Institution for the War Blinded at Linburn.

A bird in the hand

IN certain circumstances, birds in search of food become exceptionally tame, even entering the house through open windows and doors. Occasionally, we've even had wrens indoors, and trying to get them out again is a most frustrating experience. Somewhere in their ancestry there must have been a real Houdini wren, a master in the art of escapology, which passed on its prowess to succeeding generations. The phrase 'a bird in the hand' really has no relevance as far as the wren is concerned, for, try as you will, you just cannot hold on to one of the slippery little bundles of feathers if it's intent on wriggling away.

The best way of catering for the wren's feeding needs is to remember its scientific name, *Troglodytes*, for it really is a troglodyte, a frequenter of the darkest corners. Some high-protein food such as grated cheese placed under a thick bush will supply the wren's needs, and it's worth remembering that they're amongst the first birds to succumb to a really cold snap. In exceptionally bad winters, the population has been decimated within weeks. Island wrens fare rather better in their milder maritime conditions, and Scotland is well off for geographical variations of the bird, for Fair Isle and St Kilda both have their own significantly different wren populations.

Robins will occasionally come on to an outstretched hand to feed, but most are unlikely to be so confiding. There is one almost sure way, however, of getting a robin in really close, and that's to offer some mealworms, the crawly brown creatures which pet shops sometimes sell as live food for pet birds. If the prospect of a handful of squirming mealworms doesn't appeal, then a few placed out on the bird table will make any robin think it's been given an early Christmas treat.

As soon as high pressure begins to dominate the November forecasts and blanket the mornings with a white covering of rime, many birds begin to take an interest in what gardens might have to offer. Windfall apples, largely neglected since the days of autumn winds, are suddenly attacked with gusto by the blackbirds and any redwings or fieldfares which happen to discover them, though in really cold weather the frozen fruit must be gey hard on their beaks!

Birds of a feather . . .

IT'S worth remembering that birds have a particular need of feeding before going off to roost. When the weather is especially cold, a small bird will lose a disproportionately large proportion of its body weight by burning up energy reserves in order to stay warm. On chilly days, birds make themselves look much fatter, by fluffing out their feathers to increase body insulation.

Rooks occasionally pay a visit to bird-tables, but seem unlikely candidates for trying their luck at such domestic feeding arrangements. In fact, they're real opportunists, and I've watched enterprising birds pull up a string with a bit of fat at the end, and hold it down with one foot while the prize was consumed. But most winter rooks are usually too interested in farmland foraging to be bothered with the trifles put out for the smaller birds. As the light begins to fail, they gather together, often accompanied by their jackdaw relations, in immense winter flocks that pepper the fields in black. Such rowdy socialising suggests that they're having a whale of a time before heading off to bed, their apparent jollifications being the origin of old countryside lore concerning 'crows' weddings', 'parliaments' and the like. Each day the pattern is repeated; just as the light begins to fade, there's a sudden cawing uproar, then with one resolve they're off, heading towards a nearby wood for their night-time roost.

Some of our Black Isle rooks have an unusual pattern of winter feeding that takes them from their roosting place out across the waters of the Inverness Firth to feed on the other side by day. Late afternoons see them winging their way low across the waves, in decidedly un-rook-like manner, before rising and whirling in the cliff-face updraught, as if rejoicing to be over *terra firma* once more. Then, some miles away, they gather in a few favoured fields, every surrounding fence-post crowned by a sitting black shape. On frosty November afternoons, when inversion mist clings coldly to the ground, the hazy western sky reddens vividly in the sunset, providing spectacular backcloths for the aerial ongoings of a flock that consists of several thousand cawing rooks and their noisy jackdaw supporters.

November days may bring an unpleasant taste of winter yet to come, but for the birds a sheltered roost and adequate food supply are the key to survival in the months that follow.

DECEMBER

'*The wintry west extends his blast,*
And hail and rain does blaw;
Or the stormy north sends driving forth
The blinding sleet and snaw . . .'

ROBERT BURNS

OUR Scottish climate is nothing if not variable. In his 'Winter Dirge', Burns paints a bleak weather picture of December at its worst. Those whose memories are long will easily recall bad times from the past when farm roads were filled with drifting snow and land communications ground to a halt. Yet, such is the changeable nature of the end-of-year weather picture that much milder, westerly influences often prevail. 'Blinding sleet and snaw' then get no mention in the weather forecasts, and would-be Christmas skiers go about with long faces and black looks. Bereft of a good blanketing of snow, Cairngorm, Glenshee, the Lecht and Aonach Mor remain mere mountain names. But given a decent white covering, they may quickly become winter playgrounds of downhill pistes and packed car parks, with eyes focused more on the snow blanket than on the snow buntings which sometimes share the ski slopes.

Snowflake bird

SNOW buntings are real winter birds, for the males have a white camouflage plumage that adds to the snow shower effect when they rise and fall, giving them the alternative affectionate name of 'snowflakes'. They're closely related to the familiar yellow buntings of our winter farmyards, but unlike the stay-at-home yites the snow buntings descend on our shores in the autumn months from breeding grounds far to the north, spending the winter days foraging for seeds round hill slopes and along the coast.

I enjoy coming upon small groups on a winter walk, twittering

159

their way in front of me as I proceed along the beach, alighting here and there to seek out marram seeds which have dropped from the upright spears of summer. Wherever sandy shorelines provide such feeding opportunities, snow buntings can be looked for at this time along the east coast, their cheery chirruping a real give-away as they rise and descend like a snow flurry. Indeed, they may turn up in the most unexpected of places, as birdwatching rugby fans can testify, for they once had the best of both worlds when a flock landed on the pitch during a game at Murrayfield.

Dapper dipper

I'M fond of the dipper at the best of times, but if ice seals the water's edge and the splashing burn coats the overhanging branches in a frosty glaze, he has a splendid setting in which to bob and bow in his never-ending way. A dipper and his burn are never parted, except when winter weather forces a shift downstream to seek some more open flow. Even so, there's still a total attachment to the water, and at such times dippers venture into the very heart of some of our Scottish towns where rivers near the sea.

You'll often know when a dipper is present along a burn. He conveniently leaves his little white visiting card on favoured water-washed stones, for it's from them that he ventures into the icy flow. He has perfected the art of walking underwater. In fact, watching one walk right under the ice is as chilling a December countryside experience as it's possible to get. The dipper really is a dapper character, immaculately clad in chestnut and black suit and shining white dickie. He's full of surprises, too, for not only is he big brother to the wren, but he has a lovely trilling song to accompany the sound of splashing water and brighten the coldest of days. He winks endlessly to the world as he dips and bows, due to the presence of a curious pale lid that's continually drawn over the eye.

Helen B. Cruickshank paints a lovely picture of the dipper in her poem where:

> *'He keeps to the chosen stretch of his native burn,*
> *Zig-zagging, if it does, close to its shining surface,*
> *Alighting from time to time on his favourite stones,*
> *Singing and trilling, the picture of sweet content.'*

A dipper and his burn are never parted. *Scotland in Focus/Laurie Campbell.*

In the old days of water-powered country mills, the dipper was often a cheery companion to the miller, finding some damp, mossy cranny beside the creaking water wheel in which to raise its young, then bringing the whole bobbing and curtseying brood out to cheer the scene.

Hibernating hedgehogs

A change of coat like that effected by the white hare of the hills is not the only response to the rigours of the winter season. By the year's close, those countryside creatures which opt out of winter by setting their body clocks into slow motion are safely into a state of hibernation. On the dark and dreich days I must confess that I sometimes envy them their blissful state of suspended animation, for it seems an eminently sensible way to escape the worst days of the year. But I suppose there are certain drawbacks, not least the fact that you might become a meal for a predator while still in your torpid trance.

161

Misconceptions still abound about the nature of hibernation. Long ago, the Reverend Gilbert White, famed incumbent of the parish of Selborne and pioneer naturalist, was inclined to the notion that swallows hibernated at the bottom of ponds. Popular belief in squirrel hibernation remains strong, despite the fact that these bushy-tailed tree-dwellers will venture from their dreys in the shortest days to scrape in anticipation of retrieving some of the food they hid away in times of plenty.

Of hedgehog hibernation there's never any doubt, though they sometimes unwisely choose a November bonfire heap in which to curl up and are thus fated to take a far longer sleep than ever they'd intended. Others strike it really lucky, like the one I chanced upon one cold and blowy December day. He'd made a real find for his seaside hibernating place. A sailing dinghy had been removed in the autumn to the safety of the shore. With a covering tarpaulin anchored down on the ground on either side with large boulders, the effect was to create an enclosed tent around the keel. Right in the heart of this canvas cavern the spiky squatter was taking his long nap among a nest of grass and paper; as dry and snug as any hedgehog might wish to be, shielded from the wind which whistled coldly round the outside.

Hunting the wren

THE several times smaller wren is an equally cheery presence in the garden or as hide-and-seek companion on a winter woodland walk, though severe weather may remove their company. But nature has a remedy for such setbacks, and in the wren's case it's the production of huge broods to take the place of those which have perished.

Sometime publicity agent for a brand of shoe polish, and sharing the old farthing coin with the sovereign's head, 'jenny wren' has endeared itself to generations of gardeners and country folk, which makes it all the harder to account for the once widespread folklore custom of the wren hunt, when the unfortunate bird was killed and symbolically carried around a village. Possibly this English and Irish custom was an echo of some ancient rite linked with the winter solstice, and Edward Armstrong, in his fascinating book *The Folklore of Birds*, has evidence that it was imported into the South-west of Scotland (possibly from the Isle of Man), being practised last century

162

at Kirkmaiden in Galloway where the ancient ceremony was known as 'The deckan o' the wren'. Fortunately, hunting the wren is more likely these days to be a case of trying to see where the bird has disappeared to in the thickness of a garden bush or among the dead ferns of a woodland floor.

City wildfowl

WHEN bodies of water freeze over, wildfowl must shift to wherever they can maintain their aquatic lifestyle. For many this means the seashore or an exodus towards the west and the milder lands of Ireland. But for others, the easier pickings of a city park are an irresistible attraction. Surrounded by the non-stop raucous chorus of black-headed gulls (minus their black caps for the duration of the winter months, but distinguished by red bills and legs), some ducks, geese and swans are able to share man's world and cash in on the advantages which can go with it.

Duddingston Loch in Edinburgh provides encounters with winter wildfowl in a pleasant setting. On this small reed-fringed loch under the dark shadow of volcanic Arthur's Seat, many ducks flight in to

Duddingston, the Capital's rich waterfowl loch. *Scotland in Focus/Laurie Campbell.*

feed and roost. For years, Duddingston has been known for its gatherings of pochard, smart little diving ducks with chestnut brown heads and grey flanks. The vast winter pochard flocks of the past were probably linked with the concentration of related species like tufted duck and scaup at the city's Seafield sewage outlet.

Introduced greylag and Canada geese share Duddingston's waters with the ducks, while the reed beds provide a roosting place for wagtails. Edinburgh is fortunate in having such an accessible and valuable wildlife habitat, providing easy opportunities for birdwatching and familiarisation with wildfowl at close range.

At Glasgow's Hogganfield Loch, the wildfowl avail themselves of the facilities at one of the city's important recreation centres. Mallard, tufted duck and bald-pated coots share the waters and the food offerings with the resident captive flock of ornamental snow geese — and, as always, the opportunist black-headed gulls.

Berried bonanza

IF the weather has been reasonably mild and open, many garden shrubs will retain some berries right to the end of the year. There was a time when plants could only be bought bare-rooted, with the result that the potential transplanting time was limited to the season when they were dormant. Now, with the advent of container-grown plants, garden centres have a wealth of shrubs which can be planted throughout the year, even in the heart of winter, as long as the weather isn't severe or the ground frozen.

It's always worthwhile casting an eye over local gardens to see just which berry producers are attracting the birds, but it's a fair bet that it will be one of a familiar group of plants. Among the most important of all berrying shrubs for wildlife are the cotoneasters. These come in a variety of habit and size, but all produce hard red berries that are not only attractive to look at, but provide a seasonal feast for birds as well. *Cotoneaster horizontalis* has the advantage of growing flat in against a wall, so that even a small garden may manage a plant or two. In our newly laid out suburban garden outside Aberdeen, we immediately planted some *cotoneaster horizontalis* below the sitting-room window. I must confess that at the back of my mind was the hope that if waxwings should ever be in the vicinity, they might be attracted to our berry crop. In the course of time, we were not to be disappointed, for a waxwing trio once spent part of a December morning stripping the berries just outside the window.

Waxwings are unforgettable birds. Some years we see none at all; in others they're driven across the North Sea by food shortage in their native Norden in great invasions that set birdwatchers racing to see them, for you could never tire of watching such lovely creatures. About starling size, the exotic strangers have warm pinkish-brown bodies with prominent crest and bright yellow wing and tail markings, but it's the brilliance of the curious red sealing-wax wing tips that really impresses.

Before our cotoneaster-eating waxwings departed, they deposited some droppings on the window sill, containing half-digested berry pulp and numerous seeds. It's in this way that dozens of new seedlings are given a strong start in life, often appearing in lines along the base of a wall where blackbirds like to leave their little offerings. *Cotoneaster horizontalis* planted near a window or door can offer some pleasant wildlife contact as the birds set to work, stripping the berry crop.

I've watched waxwings feed on berberis and honeysuckle, and both are also excellent food plants. *Berberis darwinii* has attractive dark purple berries with a misty bloom on each, and has the advantage of producing a fine display of orange or yellow flowers earlier in the season. Cotoneaster flowers, by contrast, are fairly insignificant, the plant's crowning glory being its prolific berry crop. Berberis is a rather prickly shrub, a fact which limits its usefulness in a fairly confined garden or patio area, but once again seedlings are never in short supply after the birds have eaten the berries. For the thrushes which eagerly devour the berry crop, recycling is clearly nothing new!

Endowed with a more straggly habit, honeysuckle can be trained along a fence or over an arch, or more naturally up through the branches of a tree, just as the wild woodbine does in our broad-leaved woods. At the end of its fairly brief flowering (marked by a pervading perfume), the clustered red berries are an attraction to many birds.

The fruits of *Fuchsia magellanica* act like a magnet for blackbirds, and another useful producer of similarly pulpy fruit is *Leycesteria formosa*, a Himalayan native shrub of fairly upright habit that does well in seaside districts.

Pyracantha, the firethorn, is my own favourite garden shrub, brightening the front wall of the house and producing clusters of

Bare-branched winter trees have a powerful impact on
country places. *Douglas Willis.*

berries of pillar-box red at a time when the garden is going into
seasonal decline. Fortunately, our blackies usually leave the berries
alone till around the beginning of December — providing the weather
hasn't been too severe — so that we can enjoy the best of both worlds:
a shrub to delight the eye and provide a food source for the birds at the
same time.

Daphne mezereum is a low-growing shrub worthy of a place in
the garden for the earliness of its mauve blossom, but the red berries
which later adorn its upright stems are also very palatable. Most berry
crops are an attraction to the various members of the thrush family,
of which blackbird and song thrush are the most familiar. But harder
weather brings redwings in about the door, and even the wary fieldfare
is drawn to feed on larger berries and any surviving apples.

166

Going to seed

SOME plants are more useful as seed-producers than as berry-bearers, an example being buddleia, the butterfly bush, whose brown seedheads are always an attraction to our neighbourhood bullfinches, green-finches and goldfinches. *Potentilla fruticosa* grows four to five feet high and has yellow flowers that are irresistible to big black and yellow bumble bees when in bloom, but also draws the bullfinches to feed on its seed heads at the back end of the year.

No garden should lack at least some of the plants that provide feeding for birds, just as wild nature would have made provision for them in some form before houses and gardens were laid out. After all, every house and garden is occupying a patch that was once the preserve of wildlife in some shape or form, so if nothing else we have some moral obligation to put something back in exchange for what we've taken away!

Garden centres can offer advice on the sort of plants to select according to such things as aspect, soil type and space, for a garden should be a thing of beauty, not just a jumble of herbage. As a keen gardener myself, I believe in encouraging wildlife to come in and make use of our garden, rather than have nature take over completely as certain 'wildlife gardeners' seem to advocate. Personally, I suspect that in some cases it's just a good excuse for having a weedy patch! If, however, wildlife can be encouraged to come in and share the space, then gardening can be doubly satisfying.

Furtive futtret

STOATS are furtive creatures, but an end-of-year stoat in winter white is one of the countryside's finest sights. The stoat's real ermine coat is more fetching by far than the robe of any peer of the realm in all his furry finery. But, like the blue hares of upland places, stoats don't always don their winter camouflage, and those that do stand out in striking contrast against the dark snow-free ground.

Viewed with suspicion by folk brought up on tales of mass attacks on innocent passers-by, the stoat is a maligned creature that is beautiful to watch. Once, I saw one shin up a fence post and lay itself out in the winter sunshine, basking ecstatically in the unseasonable midday warmth. It seemed an uncomfortable kind of bed, but the stoat was clearly happy with its choice.

Their slight bodies can get them out of the narrowest of scrapes, but stoats are imbued with great strength, as anyone who has seen one drag a rabbit along the ground will confirm. And they're adaptable creatures, too, thinking nothing of taking the plunge, for I've seen them make easy work of a wide burn crossing.

A real winter stoat is a 'fyte futtret' in the North-east, though not changing its dress to suit the season may stand it in good stead for the future if the proponents of the theory of global warming are correct and lowland snow becomes a scarce Scottish commodity. I'd always though of stoats as intelligent creatures till one individual on our local golf course took to scuttling over the fairways and making off with irate players' golf balls, in the mistaken hope, presumably, of finding a tasty yoke inside.

Menacing mink

ONE autumn and winter I had the good fortune to live in a cottage next to a pond which had once served a nearby meal mill. On the whole, there seemed to be comparatively little wildlife interest about the place: a few swallows and martins hawking over the surface and a solitary water rail, but of waterhens which I would have expected, there was never any sign.

Then, one day, a likely reason for their absence became all too clear. The water was within the hunting ground of a mink, a dark furtive creature which sniffed and twitched excitedly as it regularly made its rounds. Any waterhen eggs or nest would have made a fine meal for this North American pest.

Mink are cousins to the native futtret. It's a real tragedy that mink should be present in our Scottish countryside at all, but they seem to be here to stay. The mink problem had its origin in less enlightened times when furs were much sought after, and owning a mink coat was the dream of many a woman. Mink farms sprang up all over the country, rearing the animals intensively on fish offal in batteries of small wire cages. Dilapidated mink cages may still be seen in many places, a reminder of the days when vast numbers were kept.

The trouble was that escaped animals found a niche for themselves in the countryside and went forth and multiplied exceedingly. The result now is that river courses and lochsides in many areas have paid the price for this ecological error. In the wild, mink revert to more conventional colours, though caged animals were bred in all shades to suit the whims of female fashion.

Over the years, I've had no shortage of encounters with feral mink. Some I've seen swimming, one had taken refuge up a tree, and once I saw one at full pelt (metaphorically speaking) after a small rabbit — the unspeakable pest in pursuit of the eminently edible prey, to parody Oscar Wilde.

The mink is also of the same clan as the ferret, the domesticated version of the polecat which is still widely used for rabbit trapping. Real polecats did once occur in the wild, but now any polecat seen will undoubtedly be a polecat-coloured ferret (as opposed to the commonly kept creamy-coloured ones), for these frequently turn up in the countryside, having either escaped from their cages or failed to come back out of a warren after a hunting expedition. On the isle of Mull, there's a long-established population of polecats derived from introduced ferrets, but to all intents and purposes they have become wild polecats again.

In the past I've had proud young ferreters bring their inquisitive charges to school in a carrying box, but mercifully the practice seems to have died away, which is just as well, for the pungent memory of the ferrets lingered long in the classroom air.

Christmas bird

FEW birds can be as closely associated with a particular time of year as the robin. Robins and Christmas have become so closely linked over the years that the festive season would be unthinkable without them. After all, where would the card designers be without this cheerful bird, forgetting for a moment those most un-robin-like gatherings which adorn some cards. The fact is that robins are decidedly aggressive little individuals, and certainly wouldn't relish having to share a garden, let alone a small tree branch, with a whole lot of others of their kind.

The link between the robin and the greeting card is, in fact, one

Robin, the red-breasted favourite of winter days. *Scotland in Focus/Eric Middleton.*

of the most direct Christmas connections of all, commemorating as it does the days when postmen wore red frock coats and bore the nickname of 'robin'. In folklore terms, the robin should perhaps be more associated with Easter time, for one legend has it that the bird acquired its red breast by drawing blood with a sharp spike removed from Christ's crown of thorns.

Robin song continues throughout the darkest days of winter, a cheerful contribution to the brightening morning, though I occasionally hear one singing well into the night, encouraged by the glow of nearby street lighting.

As the old year dies, and the last days on the calendar mark out the month's close, I listen for the first cheery ringing of the great tit's emerging spring song. It's a timely reminder that the year's end is but a year's beginning, and, unregulated by human calendar, the cycle of the seasons goes on, giving pulse and pattern to our Scottish country places.

APPENDIX

NATURE
RESERVES
TO
VISIT

S COTLAND is well endowed in nature reserves and a host of other special places. The table lists locales which are mentioned in the book, but there are many more which well repay a visit.

Abbreviations used in the table:

SWT — Scottish Wildlife Trust
RSPB — Royal Society for the Protection of Birds
NTS — National Trust for Scotland
NCC — Nature Conservancy Council
FC — Forestry Commission

It should be borne in mind that special visiting arrangements exist at many places, so it is important to establish in advance what these are. A stamped addressed envelope should accompany any request for information.

Useful addresses:

Scottish Wildlife Trust, 25 Johnston Terrace, Edinburgh EH1 2NH.

Royal Society for the Protection of Birds, 17 Regent Terrace, Edinburgh EH7 5BN.

National Trust for Scotland, 5 Charlotte Square, Edinburgh EH2 4DR.

Nature Conservancy Council, 12 Hope Terrace, Edinburgh EH9 2AS.

The Forestry Commission now has an impressive list of forest walks, etc. Information on these may be had from the appropriate regional office:

Forestry Commission (North Scotland), 21 Church Street, Inverness IV1 1EL.

Forestry Commission (Mid Scotland), Portcullis House, 21 India Street, Glasgow G2 4PL.

Forestry Commission (South Scotland), 55–57 Moffat Road, Dumfries DG1 1NP.

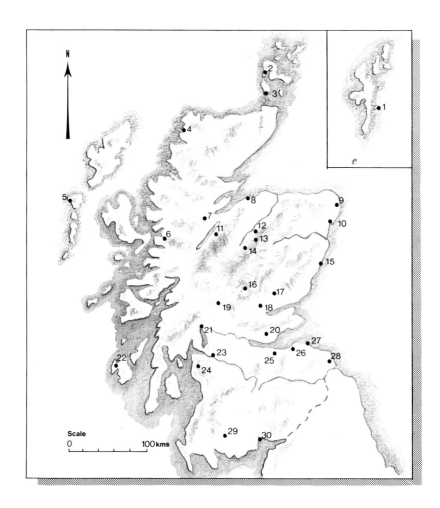

NATURE RESERVES

APPENDIX

Area tourist offices throughout Scotland have local details of nature reserves, woodland walks, etc. The Scottish Tourist Board supplies a list of tourist offices, and also publishes a useful guidebook called *Walks & Trails in Scotland*. The Board's address is:

The Scottish Tourist Board, 23 Ravelston Terrace, Edinburgh EH4 3EU.

Anyone with a particular interest in the study of birds in Scotland should consider joining the Scottish Ornithologists' Club. The SOC has winter lectures and summer outings based in several Scottish towns. The address is:

The Scottish Ornithologists' Club, 21 Regent Terrace, Edinburgh EH7 5BT.

A visit to one of the three Scottish island bird observatories can be a rewarding holiday experience. Addresses are:

Fair Isle Bird Observatory, Fair Isle Lodge, Shetland ZE2 9JU.

North Ronaldsay Bird Observatory, North Ronaldsay, Orkney KS17 2BE.

Isle of May Bird Observatory, c/o 21 Regent Terrace, Edinburgh EH7 5BT.

Suppliers of garden bird feeding and nesting equipment:

Scottish National Institution for the War Blinded, Linburn, Wilkieston, Kirknewton, Midlothian EH7 8DU.
(Nestboxes, feeding equipment).

Royal Society for the Protection of Birds, The Lodge, Sandy, Bedfordshire SG19 1BR.
(Bird tables, feeding equipment, nestboxes, etc.)

Nerine Nurseries, Welland, Near Malvern, Worcestershire WR13 6LN.
(House martin nests)

Jamie Wood Products Ltd., Cross Street, Polegate, East Sussex BN26 6BN.
(Wide range of nestboxes for small birds, owls and bats. Also bird feeding equipment, bird tables, hides, etc.)

Location

1. NOSS, Shetland. From island of Bressay via Lerwick   RSPB
    Impressive seabird colony on sandstone cliff ledges. Nesting skuas.

2. MARWICK HEAD, Orkney. West Mainland coast   RSPB
    Nesting seabirds, spectacular cliff scenery. Coastal flowers.

3. HILL OF THE WHITE HAMARS, Orkney. Island of Hoy via Stromness   SWT
    Dramatic coastline. Interesting coastal plants

4. HANDA, Highland. Private boat hire from Tarbet, West Sutherland   RSPB
    Seabirds on Torridonian Sandstone cliffs and stacks, skuas.

5. BALRANALD, Western Isles. Island of North Uist   RSPB
    Corncrakes on croftland. Birds and flowers of marsh and machair.

6. KINTAIL, Highland. Wester Ross   NTS
   Impressive mountain scenery. Red deer, wild goats.

7. GLEN AFFRIC, Highland. Via Beauly, Inverness-shire   FC
   Old Caledonian pine forest

8. CULBIN FOREST, Grampian. Access (on foot) from Cloddymoss near Dyke, between Nairn and Forres   FC
   Largest sand dune system in British Isles — now afforested. Crested tits, capercaillies and other pine forest birds. Interesting pinewood plants.

9. LOCH OF STRATHBEG, Grampian. Off main Peterhead–Fraserburgh road   RSPB
   Spectacular wildfowl gatherings, including geese and whooper swans. Lost village of Rattray.

10. SANDS OF FORVIE, Grampian. Newburgh on Ythan, north of Aberdeen   NCC
    Sand dune complex, lost village, nesting terns and eider ducks.

11. LOCH RUTHVEN, Highland. Near Loch Ness, via A9 and B851   RSPB
    Highland loch. Slavonian grebes.

12. LOCH GARTEN, Highland. Boat of Garten, off A9 near Aviemore   RSPB
    Osprey, crested tit, crossbill, capercaillie, redstart.

13. PASS OF RYVOAN, Highland. Glenmore via Aviemore   SWT
    Scree slopes with old Caledonian pines. Crossbill, crested tit, tree pipit.

14. INSH MARSHES, Highland. Off A9, near Aviemore   RSPB
    Valley marshland. Whooper swans in winter. Many nesting wildfowl. Birds of prey feeding and on passage.

15. FOWLSHEUGH, Grampian. Off A92 south of Stonehaven   RSPB
    Nesting seabirds in 'pudding stone' cliffs.

16. KILLIECRANKIE, Tayside. Off A9, near Pitlochry   RSPB
    Broad-leaved woodland in deep valley of River Garry. Warblers, pied flycatchers, woodpeckers, red squirrels. Nearby Hermitage (NTS) also has attractive woodland.

17. LOCH OF KINNORDY, Tayside. Near Kirriemuir   RSPB
    Loch and marsh. Nesting wildfowl, grebes, black-headed gulls. Wintering wildfowl.

18. LOCH OF THE LOWES, Tayside. Near Dunkeld   SWT
    Loch and marsh with woodland. Grebes, wildfowl, osprey has nested.

19. BEN LAWERS, Tayside. A827 from Aberfeldy, above Loch Tay   NTS-NCC
    Mountain and moorland area renowned for alpine/Arctic flora.

20. LOCH LEVEN (VANE FARM), Tayside. B9097 off Junction 5, M90   RSPB
    Educational centre with varied habitats. Winter geese and ducks, breeding ducks and woodland species.

21. LOCH LOMOND (INVERSNAID), Central. From Aberfoyle, east side of Loch Lomond   RSPB
    Broad-leaved woodland in attractive lochside setting up to moorland. Woodland birds, wild goats and deer.

APPENDIX

22. ISLAY (LOCH GRUINART), Strathclyde. Island of Islay   RSPB
    Farmland and saltmarsh. Barnacle and white-front geese. Short-eared owl and other birds of prey.

23. POSSIL MARSH, Strathclyde. Northern edge of Glasgow   SWT
    Marsh and open water. Sedge plants, warblers, reed buntings, migrants.

24. LOCHWINNOCH, Strathclyde. Off A760, Paisley-Largs road   RSPB
    Marsh and loch, woodland scrub. Duck, grebes, waders, wildfowl.

25. DUDDINGSTON LOCH, Lothian. Edinburgh   Scot. Dev. Dept.—SWT
    Loch and reed bed. Winter wildfowl, nesting geese.

26. ABERLADY BAY, Lothian. A198 Edinburgh-North Berwick   East Lothian DC
    Sandy bay with dunes and saltmarsh. Autumn and winter waders and wildfowl. Nesting eider, shelduck and waders.

27. BASS ROCK, Lothian. Access by arrangement with local boatman, North Berwick   Private
    Volcanic island. Huge gannet colony.

28. ST ABB'S HEAD, Borders. Off A1107, Coldingham   NTS-SWT
    Spectacular cliff scenery. Seabird colony. Bird migration lookout point.

29. KEN-DEE MARSHES, Dumfries & Galloway. Off A713 New Galloway-Castle Douglas Road   RSPB
    Marsh and waterlogged river flood plain. Wildfowl, including geese and whooper swans, grebes, hen harriers, otters.

30. CAERLAVEROCK, Dumfries & Galloway. Off B725 from Dumfries   NCC
    Coastal marsh. Barnacle and grey geese, waders.

INDEX